Diabetic Dessert Cookbook

Quick and Easy Diabetic Friendly Cakes, Pie, Tarts, Cookies, Bars, Frozen Treats, Pudding, Beverages and More, No More Hesitation

by

Master Kenri

Copyright © 2024 by Master Kenri

This book is protected by copyright law. All rights reserved. No part of this book may be reproduced, distributed, or transmitted without the publisher's prior written permission, except for brief excerpts in critical reviews and other non-commercial uses permitted by copyright law.

Table of Contents

INTRODUCTION TO DIABETIC DESSERTS — 7

UNDERSTANDING DIABETES AND DESSERTS — 9

ESSENTIAL INGREDIENTS FOR DIABETIC DESSERTS — 11

TIPS FOR SUGAR SUBSTITUTION AND SWEETENERS — 13

TOOLS AND EQUIPMENT FOR DIABETIC BAKING — 15

DECADENT CAKES AND CUPCAKES — 17

- VANILLA ALMOND CAKE — 17
- CHOCOLATE AVOCADO CUPCAKES — 17
- LEMON YOGURT CAKE — 18
- FLOURLESS CHOCOLATE CAKE — 19
- CREAM CHEESE FROSTED CARROT CAKE — 20
- RASPBERRY ALMOND FLOUR CAKE — 21
- COCONUT FLOUR POUND CAKE — 22
- RED VELVET BEET CAKE — 23
- ORANGE OLIVE OIL CAKE — 24
- ALMOND JOY CUPCAKES — 24
- ESPRESSO CHOCOLATE CAKE — 25
- PUMPKIN SPICE CAKE — 26
- BANANA WALNUT CAKE WITH GREEK YOGURT FROSTING — 27
- BLACK FOREST CUPCAKES — 28
- PINEAPPLE COCONUT CAKE — 29

DELICIOUS PIES AND TARTS — 31

- SUGAR-FREE APPLE PIE — 31
- BERRY ALMOND TART — 31
- KEY LIME PIE WITH ALMOND CRUST — 32
- PUMPKIN PIE WITH PECAN CRUST — 33
- LEMON BLUEBERRY TART — 33
- PEACH RASPBERRY GALETTE — 34

Chocolate Pecan Pie Bars	35
Coconut Cream Pie	36
Strawberry Rhubarb Crisp	37
Mini Lemon Meringue Pies	37
Mixed Berry Galette	38
Almond Flour Apple Tart	39
Cherry Almond Crumble	40
Maple Walnut Pie	40
Chocolate Silk Tart	41

INDULGENT COOKIES AND BARS 43

Oatmeal Raisin Cookies	43
Peanut Butter Chocolate Chip Bars	43
Almond Flour Shortbread Cookies	44
Chocolate Walnut Brownies	45
Cranberry Orange Biscotti	46
Maple Pecan Bars	46
Coconut Macaroons	47
Espresso Chocolate Chunk Cookies	48
Lemon Poppy Seed Bars	49
Ginger Molasses Cookies	49
Pistachio Cranberry Biscotti	50
Chocolate Hazelnut Biscotti	51
Blueberry Oatmeal Bars	52
Pumpkin Chocolate Chip Cookies	53
Apricot Almond Bars	54

FROZEN TREATS AND POPSICLES 55

Strawberry Greek Yogurt Popsicles	55
Avocado Lime Sorbet	55
Chocolate Banana Nice Cream	56
Mango Coconut Ice Pops	57
Blueberry Basil Sorbet	57
Pineapple Mint Granita	58
Raspberry Swirl Frozen Yogurt	59
Kiwi Lime Popsicles	59
Watermelon Mint Sorbet	60
Peach Yogurt Ice Pops	60
Coconut Lime Popsicles	61

CHERRY VANILLA FROZEN YOGURT	62
PINEAPPLE COCONUT SORBET	63
RASPBERRY MANGO SORBET	63
HONEYDEW MINT ICE POPS	64

GUILT-FREE PUDDINGS AND CUSTARDS — 65

CHIA SEED PUDDING	65
COCONUT MILK RICE PUDDING	65
PUMPKIN SPICE CUSTARD	66
CHOCOLATE AVOCADO PUDDING	67
VANILLA BEAN TAPIOCA PUDDING	67
MATCHA GREEN TEA PUDDING	68
ALMOND JOY CHIA PUDDING	68
CINNAMON MAPLE RICE PUDDING	69
LEMON COCONUT CUSTARD CUPS	70
ESPRESSO CHOCOLATE POTS DE CRÈME	70
STRAWBERRY CHIA PUDDING	71
BLUEBERRY COCONUT RICE PUDDING	72
CHOCOLATE PEANUT BUTTER CHIA PUDDING	73
MANGO COCONUT TAPIOCA PUDDING	73
RASPBERRY ALMOND CUSTARD	74

SWEETENED BEVERAGES AND MOCKTAILS — 75

SPARKLING BERRY LEMONADE	75
MINTY ICED GREEN TEA	75
CUCUMBER LIME COOLER	76
WATERMELON BASIL LEMONADE	77
PEACH GINGER MOCKTAIL	77
BLUEBERRY LAVENDER LEMONADE	78
RASPBERRY MINT ICED TEA	79
PINEAPPLE COCONUT REFRESHER	80
CRANBERRY ORANGE SPRITZER	80
HONEYDEW MINT COOLER	81
STRAWBERRY BASIL LEMONADE	81
MANGO PINEAPPLE PUNCH	82
KIWI COCONUT COOLER	83
BLACKBERRY MINT MOCKTAIL	83
GRAPEFRUIT ROSEMARY SPRITZER	84

SPECIAL OCCASION DESSERTS: 86

- Flourless Chocolate Torte _____ 86
- Tiramisu Parfaits _____ 86
- Raspberry Swirl Cheesecake _____ 87
- Chocolate-Dipped Strawberries _____ 88
- Red Velvet Cake Bites _____ 88
- Hazelnut Mousse with Dark Chocolate Drizzle _____ 89
- Lemon Blueberry Trifle _____ 90
- Pistachio Rosewater Semifreddo _____ 91
- Coconut Cream Pie with Almond Crust _____ 91
- Salted Caramel Chocolate Pots de Crème _____ 92

BONUS RECIPES 94

- Sugar-Free Vanilla Frosting _____ 94
- Cream Cheese Frosting with Stevia _____ 94
- Homemade Whipped Cream with Coconut Milk _____ 95
- Dark Chocolate Ganache _____ 95
- Fresh Fruit Compote _____ 96
- Sugar-Free Caramel Sauce _____ 96
- Lemon Glaze with Monk Fruit Sweetener _____ 97
- Chocolate Avocado Mousse _____ 98
- Almond Buttercream Frosting _____ 98
- Vanilla Bean Pastry Cream _____ 99

CONCLUSION AND FINAL TIPS FOR DIABETIC DESSERT SUCCESS 100

Introduction to Diabetic Desserts

Welcome to the delicious world of desserts for diabetics, where enjoyment meets moderation and flavor meets responsibility. In this chapter, we set out to rethink dessert as something that people with Diabetes can enjoy. The days of limitation and deprivation are long gone, and in their place is a new paradigm of culinary innovation that allows sweets to be consciously and guilt-free enjoyed.

EMBRACING DESSERTS WITH DIABETES

SHIFTING PERSPECTIVES:
They are urging readers to reconsider their relationship with sweets and see them as chances for gastronomic inquiry and enjoyment rather than as banned foods.

EMPOWERING CHOICES:
They are giving people with Diabetes the tools they need to make educated choices regarding dessert intake by stressing moderation, balance, and individual preference.

UNDERSTANDING THE DIABETES-DESSERT CONNECTION

DIABETES DEMYSTIFIED:
We are presenting an extensive review of Diabetes, covering its causes, kinds, and effects on blood sugar regulation.

IMPACT OF DESSERTS:
They are examining how classic desserts, with their high sugar and carbohydrate content and ability to interfere with blood sugar regulation, present issues for people with Diabetes.

THE PROMISE OF DIABETIC-FRIENDLY DESSERTS

SWEET WITHOUT SACRIFICE:
Let me introduce you to the idea of diabetic-friendly sweets, which fit the dietary requirements of people with Diabetes while emphasizing flavor, texture, and satisfaction.

ACT OF BALANCE:
It highlights the significance of nutrient-dense ingredients, controlling portion sizes, reducing sugar content, and stressing the necessity of balance in diabetic dessert recipes.

HOW TO USE THE COOKBOOK

EXAMINING THE DISHES:
Get a sneak peek at the wide range of diabetic-friendly dessert dishes in the cookbook, which includes anything from pies and frozen desserts to cakes and cookies.

ADVICE AND METHODS:
We are providing advice on recipe adjustments, ingredient swaps, and baking techniques to improve blood sugar management and improve cooking performance.

Understanding Diabetes and Desserts

We explore the mutually beneficial relationship between desserts and Diabetes. For those who are managing Diabetes, it is crucial to comprehend the complex dynamics of blood sugar management and the influence of food choices on glucose levels. Let's examine the intricacies, difficulties, and methods for indulging in sweets without compromising health.

DIABETES DEMYSTIFIED

TYPES OF DIABETES:
A thorough explanation of Type 1, Type 2, gestational Diabetes, and prediabetes, along with an emphasis on their unique traits and effects.

BASICS OF BLOOD SUGAR:
We are examining the processes underlying blood sugar homeostasis, with an emphasis on the function of insulin and how Diabetes upsets this balance.

THE SWEET CONUNDRUM: DESSERTS AND DIABETES

UNDERSTANDING SUGAR'S IMPACT:
They are investigating the damaging effects that conventional sweets that are high in sugar and refined carbs can have on blood sugar levels.

CARB AWARENESS:
They are shedding light on the relationship between the amount of carbohydrates in desserts and the glycemic response.

NAVIGATING THE DESERT LANDSCAPE

GLYCEMIC INDEX AND LOAD:
A thorough breakdown of GI and GL enables readers to choose desserts wisely depending on how they affect blood sugar.

SUGAR SUBSTITUTES:
A look at several other sweeteners and how they can help make treats that are diabetic-friendly without compromising flavor.

STRATEGIES FOR SAVVY DESSERT CONSUMPTION

TECHNIQUES FOR PORTION CONTROL:
Helpful advice for controlling portion sizes to reduce blood sugar rises and sate cravings for sweets.

BALANCED EATING HABITS:
I am stressing the significance of including desserts in a comprehensive meal plan in order to preserve blood sugar stability.

MONITORING AND MANAGING

BLOOD SUGAR MONITORING:
Instructions on how to take accurate measurements, monitor blood sugar levels, and modify dessert intake as necessary.

LIFESTYLE MODIFICATIONS:
Techniques for combining regular exercise with stress reduction to support dietary efforts in the control of Diabetes.

EXPLORING DIABETIC-FRIENDLY DESSERTS

MODIFICATIONS TO THE RECIPE:
Methods for modifying classic dessert recipes, such as cutting the sugar content and adding whole grains, to make them diabetes-friendly.

TEMPTING SUBSTITUTES:
They are introducing a variety of dessert alternatives that are suitable for people with Diabetes to satiate a range of desires, from decadent cakes to cool frozen desserts.

EDUCATING AND EMPOWERING

MYTH BUSTING:
Clearing up frequent misunderstandings and myths about sweets and Diabetes to enable readers to make wise decisions.

PROMOTING DIABETES AWARENESS:
Promoting diabetes awareness and de-stigmatization through advocacy can help create a community that is supportive of those who are managing the illness.

COLLABORATING WITH CARE

PARTNERING WITH HEALTHCARE PROFESSIONALS:
We are emphasizing the need to consult with diabetes educators, certified dietitians, and medical professionals to customize dietary plans for specific requirements.

Readers are more prepared to handle the challenges of controlling blood sugar while indulging in the delights of sweet foods, thanks to their expanded knowledge of Diabetes and the dynamics of desserts. People with Diabetes can embrace a satisfying dessert experience that nourishes both body and soul by combining information, awareness, and collaboration.

Essential Ingredients for Diabetic Desserts

We look at the key components that make up diabetic-friendly dessert recipes. People with Diabetes can make delectable desserts that fit their nutritional requirements and improve blood sugar control by knowing the functions of each ingredient and how to replace conventional items with healthy alternatives.

FLOUR ALTERNATIVES

ALMOND FLOUR:
A nutrient-dense, adaptable substitute for regular wheat flour, almond flour gives baked goods a moist texture and subtle nutty flavor while cutting down on the amount of carbohydrates.

COCONUT FLOUR:
If you're looking to reduce the total amount of carbohydrates in your sweets, coconut flour is an excellent option because of its high fiber content and low glycemic index.

NATURAL SWEETENERS

STEVIA:
The naturally occurring sweetener stevia is derived from the leaves of the Stevia rebaudiana plant and has no calories. It is an excellent substitute for sugar in diabetic treats since it adds sweetness without increasing blood sugar.

EXTRACT FROM MONK FRUIT:
This non-nutritive sweetener is made from monk fruit and tastes sweet without having the same glycemic impact as sugar, so those with Diabetes can use it.

HEALTHY FATS

AVOCADO:
Packed with fiber and heart-healthy monounsaturated fats, avocados give sweets a creamy, luscious texture while also supplying vital nutrients and encouraging fullness.

COCONUT OIL:
Adding a hint of coconut flavor and lowering the glycemic impact, coconut oil is a tasty and stable fat substitute that may be used in place of butter or other oils in recipes.

WHOLE GRAINS

OATMEAL:
Oats are a diabetic-friendly substitute for refined grains because they are high in soluble fiber and complex carbs, which help regulate blood sugar levels and support digestive health.

QUINOA:
Quinoa is a grain that is free of gluten and whole protein. It gives sweets texture and nutritional value and has a low glycemic index.

LOW-GLYCEMIC FRUITS

BERRIES:
Berries, such as raspberries, strawberries, and blueberries, are low in sugar and high in fiber, vitamins, and antioxidants. They can be used as sweets to give them a naturally sweet taste and colorful appearance.

CITRUS FRUITS:
Citrus fruits, such as lemons and limes, add pizzazz to desserts with their tart flavor and high vitamin C content, all without significantly raising blood sugar levels.

NUTRITIOUS ADD-INS

NUTS AND SEEDS:
Rich in protein, fiber, and good fats, nuts and seeds like chia seeds, walnuts, and almonds give diabetic treats a crunch, texture, and nutritional boost.

UNSWEETENED COCOA POWDER:
Packed with natural components and antioxidants, unsweetened cocoa powder gives sweets a rich chocolate flavor without the additional sugars of store-bought cocoa blends.

DAIRY AND DAIRY ALTERNATIVES

GREEK YOGURT:
Rich in probiotics and protein, Greek yogurt gives desserts a creamy, tangy taste while supplying vital nutrients and supporting digestive health.

UNSWEETENED ALMOND MILK:
To cut down on carbohydrates and boost the taste in dishes, use unsweetened almond milk instead of ordinary milk. It's a low-calorie, dairy-free substitute for cow's milk.

Tips for Sugar Substitution and Sweeteners

We examine the science and art of substituting sugar and other sweeteners in sweets that are suitable for people with Diabetes. People with Diabetes can still enjoy the sweetness of desserts without sacrificing blood sugar control if they know the characteristics of different sweeteners and how to use them in place of sugar.

UNDERSTANDING SUGAR AND ITS IMPACT

THE ROLE OF SUGAR:
A brief synopsis of the function of sugar in baking and how it affects blood sugar levels, with a focus on moderation and thoughtful consumption.

RISKS OF EXCESS SUGAR INTAKE:
We are examining the harmful effects of overeating sugar on one's health, such as obesity, insulin resistance, and an elevated risk of developing complications from Diabetes.

CHOOSING THE RIGHT SWEETENERS

NATURAL SWEETENERS:
They are introducing sugar-free alternatives to sugar that taste sweet without the calories or carbs. Examples of these are erythritol, stevia, and monk fruit extract.

ARTIFICIAL SWEETENERS:
Sweeteners such as aspartame, sucralose, and saccharin provide an intense sweetness without significantly affecting blood sugar levels.

FACTORS TO CONSIDER WHEN SUBSTITUTING SUGAR

SWEETNESS LEVEL:
To get the right amount of sweetness, recipes should be adjusted based on how sweeteners compare to sugar in terms of relative sweetness.

TEXTURE AND MOISTURE:
Making the necessary modifications to preserve the proper consistency requires taking into account how sweeteners affect the texture and moisture content of baked goods.

EXPERIMENTING WITH BLENDS

BLENDING SWEETENERS:
Examining the possible advantages of combining several sweeteners to promote sweetness, balanced flavor profiles, and reduce aftertaste.

CUSTOMIZING FLAVOR PROFILES:
Experiment with spices, flavor extracts, and other substances to enhance each sweetener's distinct flavor and produce mouthwatering flavor combinations.

TIPS FOR SUCCESSFUL SUGAR SUBSTITUTION

RECIPE MODIFICATION:
This section offers instructions on how to change classic recipes so that alternative sweeteners can be used in place of sugar, including changing ingredient amounts and baking times.

TASTE TESTS:
Advising readers to sample pastries while they're baking to make sure the sweetness and flavor are balanced just right.

NAVIGATING LABELING AND PACKAGING

READING FOOD LABELS:
Teaching consumers how to scan food labels for hidden sugars and make decisions about reduced-sugar or alternative sweetener products.

IDENTIFYING SUGAR ALCOHOLS:
Highlighting the possible gastrointestinal effects of common sugar alcohols such as erythritol, xylitol, and maltitol when ingested in excess.

INCORPORATING SWEETENERS INTO EVERYDAY LIFE

BEYOND BAKING:
Inventive methods for using sugar substitutes in regular recipes and drinks, like dressings, sauces, and beverages.

MINDFUL CONSUMPTION:
Stressing that while using alternative sweeteners, portion control and mindfulness is crucial because overindulging can still have an adverse effect on blood sugar levels.

Tools and Equipment for Diabetic Baking

We go into the fundamental supplies and machinery that will enable people to start making delectable desserts that are suitable for people with Diabetes. Having the appropriate tools at your disposal can make all the difference in the success of your dessert attempts, from specialist baking equipment to precision measuring instruments.

BASIC KITCHEN ESSENTIALS

MEASURING CUPS AND SPOONS:
Accurate ingredient portioning in baking requires precision, so get a set of sturdy measuring cups and spoons.

MIXING BOWLS:
When preparing dessert dishes, having a range of mixing bowls in various sizes ensures convenience and versatility.

WHISKS & SPATULAS:
An essential toolkit for every baker is comprised of whisks for combining ingredients seamlessly and spatulas for scraping down bowls.

BAKING ESSENTIALS

OVEN THERMOMETER:
To ensure precise baking temperatures and reliable outcomes, use an oven thermometer to calibrate your oven correctly.

BAKING SHEETS AND PANS:
To suit a variety of dessert recipes and baking requirements, get a selection of baking sheets, cake pans, and muffin tins.

COOLING RACKS:
After baking, move pastries to wire cooling racks to allow them to cool uniformly and avoid becoming soggy.

SPECIALIZED EQUIPMENT FOR DIABETIC-FRIENDLY DESSERTS

BLENDER OR FOOD PROCESSOR:
Necessary for blending components for diabetic-friendly dessert recipes, such as fillings and crusts, and for making smooth purees and grinding nuts.

IMMERSION BLENDER:
Perfect for smoothing out textures in custards, puddings, and sauces without requiring hot liquids to be transferred to a conventional blender.

THE MICROPLANE OR ZESTER:
Using a zester or microplane, add grated spices, chocolate shavings, or citrus zest to sweets to give them bursts of flavor.

ALTERNATIVE SWEETENER DISPENSERS

STEVIA DROPPER:
A dropper container allows you to precisely and controllably dispense liquid stevia, guaranteeing precise sweetness levels without spilling too much.

MONK SHAKER FOR FRUIT POWDER:
Store monk fruit powder in a shaker so you can easily add it to desserts, drinks, and snacks for a convenient way to sweeten them.

STORAGE AND PRESERVATION

CONTAINERS THAT ARE AIRTIGHT:
Baked goods should be kept out of the air and away from moisture to maintain their freshness and flavor.

BAGS OR CONTAINERS FOR FREEZER:
Desserts can have a longer shelf life if you freeze individual servings in freezer bags or containers, which will make it simple to thaw and enjoy them later.

Decadent Cakes and Cupcakes

Vanilla Almond Cake

INGREDIENTS:
- All-purpose flour: 2 cups
- Almond flour: 1 cup
- Baking powder: 2 teaspoons
- Salt: 1/2 teaspoon
- Unsalted butter, softened: 1 cup
- Granulated sugar: 1 1/2 cups
- Eggs: 4 large
- Vanilla extract: 2 teaspoons
- Almond extract: 1 teaspoon
- Milk: 1 cup

INSTRUCTIONS:
- Turn the oven on to 350°F or 175°C, and dust a 9-inch cake pan with flour.
- Mix the almond flour, baking powder, salt, and all-purpose flour in a medium-sized bowl.
- Beat the butter and sugar in a sizable mixing basin until they are light and creamy.
- One egg at a time, adding and beating thoroughly after each addition. Add the almond and vanilla extracts and stir.
- Add the dry ingredients to the wet ingredients gradually, starting and finishing with the dry ingredients and alternating with the milk.
- Fill the cake pan with batter; bake for 35 to 40 minutes or until a toothpick inserted in the middle comes out clean.
- After letting the cake set in the pan for ten minutes, move it to a wire rack to finish cooling.

NUTRITION PLAN FOR DIABETICS:
This cake is ideal for those with Diabetes because it has less sugar than typical cakes. The addition of fiber and good fats from the almond flour may aid in normalizing blood sugar levels.

SHAPES AND BENEFITS:
Easily sliced, whether baked in a loaf pan or as a round cake. Rich in protein, fiber, and good fats, almonds can lower blood sugar and strengthen heart health.

Chocolate Avocado Cupcakes

INGREDIENTS:
- Ripe avocados: 2 medium

- ◇ Unsweetened cocoa powder: 1/2 cup
- ◇ Eggs: 2 large
- ◇ Honey or maple syrup: 1/2 cup
- ◇ Vanilla extract: 1 teaspoon
- ◇ Almond flour: 1/2 cup
- ◇ Baking soda: 1 teaspoon
- ◇ Salt: 1/4 teaspoon

INSTRUCTIONS:

◇ Heat the oven to 350°F (175°C) and place cupcake liners inside a muffin tray.

◇ Process the avocados in a food processor until smooth.

◇ In the food processor, add the eggs, vanilla extract, honey (or maple syrup), and cocoa powder. Process until thoroughly blended.

◇ Mix the baking soda, salt, and almond flour in another basin.

◇ Add the dry ingredients to the avocado mixture gradually and stir until well combined.

◇ Using cupcake liners that have been prepared, divide the batter equally.

◇ When a toothpick put into the center comes out clean, bake for 18 to 20 minutes.

◇ After letting the cupcakes cool in the pan for five minutes, move them to a wire rack to finish cooling.

NUTRITION PLAN FOR DIABETICS:

Compared to regular cupcakes, these have less sugar and carbs, making them a healthier choice for people with Diabetes. The addition of fiber and good fats from the avocado can help control blood sugar levels and increase feelings of fullness.

SHAPES AND BENEFITS:

Because cupcakes provide for easy single servings, portion control is much simpler. Rich in fiber and monounsaturated fats, avocados can lower the risk of heart disease and increase insulin sensitivity.

Lemon Yogurt Cake

INGREDIENTS:

- ◇ All-purpose flour: 1 1/2 cups
- ◇ Baking powder: 2 teaspoons
- ◇ Salt: 1/4 teaspoon
- ◇ Unsalted butter, softened: 1/2 cup
- ◇ Granulated sugar: 1 cup
- ◇ Eggs: 3 large
- ◇ Plain Greek yogurt: 1 cup
- ◇ Lemon zest: 2 tablespoons
- ◇ Lemon juice: 1/4 cup

◇ Vanilla extract: 1 teaspoon

INSTRUCTIONS:

◇ Heat the oven to 350°F (175°C). Lightly coat a 9x5-inch loaf pan with flour and butter.
◇ Whisk the flour, baking powder, and salt in a medium-sized bowl.
◇ Beat the butter and sugar in a sizable mixing basin until they are light and creamy.
◇ One egg at a time, adding and beating thoroughly after each addition. Add the Greek yogurt, vanilla essence, lemon zest, and lemon juice and stir.
◇ Mix until just incorporated, and gradually add the dry ingredients to the wet ones.
◇ Using a spatula, level the top of the batter once it has been poured into the loaf pan.
◇ When a toothpick put into the center comes out clean, bake for 45 to 50 minutes.
◇ After letting the cake set in the pan for ten minutes, move it to a wire rack to finish cooling.

NUTRITION PLAN FOR DIABETICS:
Compared to regular cakes, this cake has less sugar, and the addition of protein and probiotics from Greek yogurt can aid in maintaining intestinal health and stabilize blood sugar levels.

SHAPES AND BENEFITS:
Easy to slice after baking in a loaf pan, it's the ideal treat to go with a cup of tea or coffee. Antioxidants and vitamin C, which are abundant in lemons, can help lower inflammation and increase insulin sensitivity.

Flourless Chocolate Cake

INGREDIENTS:

◇ Dark chocolate (at least 70% cocoa): 8 ounces
◇ Unsalted butter: 1/2 cup
◇ Granulated sugar or sweetener of choice: 3/4 cup
◇ Eggs: 4 large
◇ Unsweetened cocoa powder: 1/4 cup
◇ Salt: 1/4 teaspoon

INSTRUCTIONS:

◇ Grease an 8-inch round cake pan and preheat the oven to 350°F (175°C).
◇ Melt the butter and dark chocolate together in a heatproof bowl over a pot of simmering water, stirring to ensure smoothness. Take off the heat and allow to cool a little.
◇ Mix the eggs, sugar or sweetener, cocoa powder, and salt thoroughly in another bowl.

- Pour the melted chocolate mixture into the egg mixture gradually while continuing to whisk until the mixture is smooth and thoroughly mixed.
- Using a spatula, level the top of the batter after pouring it into the prepared cake pan.
- Bake for 25 to 30 minutes, or until the center is still jiggly, but the edges are set.
- Take out of the oven and allow it to cool fully in the pan using a wire rack.
- After the cake has cooled, remove it from the pan by running a knife around the sides. Turn over onto a platter.

NUTRITION PLAN FOR DIABETICS:
This flourless cake is naturally low in carbohydrates and gluten, making it a good choice for people with Diabetes. Antioxidants found in dark chocolate may enhance insulin sensitivity.

SHAPES AND BENEFITS:
This cake, when baked in a round cake pan, has a dense, decadent texture. Due to its heart-healthy properties, dark chocolate may lower the risk of cardiovascular disease.

Cream Cheese Frosted Carrot Cake

INGREDIENTS:
- All-purpose flour: 1 1/2 cups
- Baking powder: 1 teaspoon
- Baking soda: 1/2 teaspoon
- Ground cinnamon: 1 teaspoon
- Salt: 1/4 teaspoon
- Unsweetened applesauce: 1/2 cup
- Vegetable oil: 1/4 cup
- Granulated sugar or sweetener of choice: 3/4 cup
- Eggs: 2 large
- Vanilla extract: 1 teaspoon
- Grated carrots: 2 cups
- Chopped nuts (optional): 1/2 cup
- Cream cheese frosting: Prepared or homemade

INSTRUCTIONS:
- Warm up the oven to 350°F (175°C) and dust a 9-inch circular cake pan with flour.
- Mix the flour, baking soda, baking powder, cinnamon, and salt in a medium-sized basin.
- Combine the eggs, sugar, vanilla extract, vegetable oil, and applesauce in a sizable mixing basin. Blend until thoroughly blended.
- Mix until just incorporated, and gradually add the dry ingredients to the wet ones.
- If using, mix in the chopped nuts and grated carrots.

◇ Using a spatula, level the top of the batter after pouring it into the prepared cake pan.
◇ When a toothpick put into the center comes out clean, bake for 25 to 30 minutes.
◇ After letting the cake set in the pan for ten minutes, move it to a wire rack to finish cooling.
◇ Apply cream cheese frosting to the cake after it has cooled.

NUTRITION PLAN FOR DIABETICS:
Carrots include fiber and nutrients that can help control blood sugar levels, and this carrot cake can be made with less sugar or other sweets.

SHAPES AND BENEFITS:
This cake is a traditional favorite, baked in a circular cake pan and topped with cream cheese icing. Beta-carotene, which is abundant in carrots, may help increase insulin sensitivity.

Raspberry Almond Flour Cake

INGREDIENTS:
◇ Almond flour: 2 cups
◇ Baking powder: 1 teaspoon
◇ Salt: 1/4 teaspoon
◇ Unsalted butter, softened: 1/2 cup
◇ Granulated sugar or sweetener of choice: 1/2 cup
◇ Eggs: 3 large
◇ Vanilla extract: 1 teaspoon
◇ Almond extract: 1/2 teaspoon
◇ Plain Greek yogurt: 1/2 cup
◇ Fresh raspberries: 1 cup

INSTRUCTIONS:
◇ Warm up the oven to 350°F (175°C) and dust a 9-inch circular cake pan with flour.
◇ Mix the baking powder, salt, and almond flour in a medium-sized bowl.
◇ Beat the butter and sugar in a sizable mixing basin until they are light and creamy.
◇ One egg at a time, adding and beating thoroughly after each addition. Add the almond and vanilla extracts and stir.
◇ Add the dry components to the wet ingredients gradually, starting and finishing with the dry ingredients and alternating with the Greek yogurt.
◇ Add the fresh raspberries and fold gently.
◇ Using a spatula, level the top of the batter after pouring it into the prepared cake pan.
◇ When a toothpick put into the center comes out clean, bake for 30 to 35 minutes.

◇ After letting the cake set in the pan for ten minutes, move it to a wire rack to finish cooling.

NUTRITION PLAN FOR DIABETICS:
Almond flour, which has less carbohydrates than wheat flour but more protein and good fats, is used to make this cake. Because they are high in fiber and low in sugar, raspberries are a fruit that is suitable for people with Diabetes.

SHAPES AND BENEFITS:
Packed with fresh raspberries for a burst of color and flavor, this cake bakes up beautifully in a round cake pan. If you have a gluten sensitivity or celiac illness, almond flour is a great gluten-free choice that adds richness and nuttiness.

Coconut Flour Pound Cake

INGREDIENTS:
◇ Coconut flour: 1 cup
◇ Baking powder: 1 teaspoon
◇ Salt: 1/4 teaspoon
◇ Unsalted butter, softened: 1/2 cup
◇ Granulated sugar or sweetener of choice: 1/2 cup
◇ Eggs: 4 large
◇ Coconut milk: 1/2 cup
◇ Vanilla extract: 1 teaspoon
◇ Shredded coconut (optional): 1/2 cup

INSTRUCTIONS:
◇ Heat the oven to 350°F (175°C). Lightly coat a 9x5-inch loaf pan with flour and butter.
◇ Mix the baking powder, salt, and coconut flour in a medium-sized bowl.
◇ Beat the butter and sugar in a sizable mixing basin until they are light and creamy.
◇ One egg at a time, adding and beating thoroughly after each addition. Add the vanilla essence and coconut milk and stir.
◇ Mixing until smooth, gradually incorporate the dry ingredients into the wet ones.
◇ If using, mix in the shredded coconut.
◇ Using a spatula, level the top of the batter once it has been poured into the loaf pan.
◇ When a toothpick put into the center comes out clean, bake for 40 to 45 minutes.
◇ After letting the cake set in the pan for ten minutes, move it to a wire rack to finish cooling.

DIETARY GUIDELINES FOR DIABETES:

When compared to wheat flour, coconut flour has less carbohydrates and more fiber, which makes it a better choice for people with Diabetes. Richness and flavor are added by coconut milk, which also contains good fats that can help control blood sugar.

SHAPES AND BENEFITS:
This pound cake tastes excellent sliced and served with a cup of tea or coffee after baking it in a loaf pan. The cake has a soft crumb with a hint of coconut flavor from the coconut flour, which makes it a delightful and filling dessert.

Red Velvet Beet Cake

INGREDIENTS:
- Cooked beets, pureed: 1 cup
- Eggs: 2 large
- Granulated sugar or sweetener of choice: 3/4 cup
- Vegetable oil: 1/2 cup
- Vanilla extract: 1 teaspoon
- All-purpose flour: 1 1/4 cups
- Unsweetened cocoa powder: 1/4 cup
- Baking powder: 1 teaspoon
- Salt: 1/4 teaspoon
- Red food coloring (optional): 1-2 tablespoons

INSTRUCTIONS:
- To make an 8-inch round cake pan, grease and flour it and preheat the oven to 350°F (175°C).
- The pureed beets, eggs, sugar, vegetable oil, and vanilla extract should all be combined in a large mixing basin. Blend until thoroughly blended.
- Sift the flour, baking powder, cocoa powder, and salt in a separate bowl.
- Mixing until smooth, gradually incorporate the dry ingredients into the wet ones.
- Add more red food coloring as needed to get the appropriate shade of red.
- Using a spatula, level the top of the batter after pouring it into the prepared cake pan.
- When a toothpick put into the center comes out clean, bake for 25 to 30 minutes.
- After letting the cake set in the pan for ten minutes, move it to a wire rack to finish cooling.

NUTRITION PLAN FOR DIABETICS:
Beets are a nutrient-dense addition to this cake because they are high in fiber, vitamins, and minerals and low in calories. Beets are a natural sweetener that can be used to lessen the need for added sugars.

SHAPES AND BENEFITS:

This cake is delicious and bright red after baking in a round cake pan. Because of their high antioxidant content and potential to lower inflammation and enhance blood flow, beets may be beneficial to people with Diabetes.

Orange Olive Oil Cake

INGREDIENTS:
- All-purpose flour: 1 1/2 cups
- Baking powder: 1 teaspoon
- Salt: 1/4 teaspoon
- Eggs: 3 large
- Granulated sugar or sweetener of choice: 1 cup
- Extra virgin olive oil: 1/2 cup
- Fresh orange juice: 1/2 cup
- Orange zest: 2 tablespoons
- Vanilla extract: 1 teaspoon

INSTRUCTIONS:
- Warm up the oven to 350°F (175°C) and dust a 9-inch circular cake pan with flour.
- Whisk the flour, baking powder, and salt in a medium-sized bowl.
- Beat the eggs and sugar in a sizable mixing basin until light and airy.
- Add the vanilla essence, fresh orange juice, orange zest, and olive oil gradually and whisk until thoroughly blended.
- Mixing until smooth, gradually incorporate the dry ingredients into the wet ones.
- Using a spatula, level the top of the batter after pouring it into the prepared cake pan.
- When a toothpick put into the center comes out clean, bake for 25 to 30 minutes.
- After letting the cake set in the pan for ten minutes, move it to a wire rack to finish cooling.

NUTRITION PLAN FOR DIABETICS:
Olive oil is a heart-healthy fat that can lower inflammation and help raise cholesterol. Oranges are a great source of antioxidants and vitamin C, which can boost immunity and reduce the risk of chronic illnesses.

SHAPES AND BENEFITS:
This cake, when baked in a round cake pan, has a vibrant citrus taste and a soft crumb. Fresh orange juice and zest provide a burst of freshness, and olive oil provides moisture and richness.

Almond Joy Cupcakes

INGREDIENTS:
- Almond flour: 1 1/2 cups

- Baking powder: 1 teaspoon
- Salt: 1/4 teaspoon
- Unsweetened cocoa powder: 1/4 cup
- Granulated sugar or sweetener of choice: 1/2 cup
- Eggs: 3 large
- Coconut milk: 1/2 cup
- Coconut oil, melted: 1/4 cup
- Vanilla extract: 1 teaspoon
- Shredded coconut (unsweetened): 1/2 cup
- Chopped almonds: 1/2 cup
- Dark chocolate chips (optional): 1/4 cup

INSTRUCTIONS:
- Heat the oven to 350°F (175°C) and place cupcake liners inside a muffin tray.
- Mix the cocoa powder, baking powder, salt, and almond flour in a medium-sized bowl.
- Mix the sugar, eggs, coconut milk, melted coconut oil, and vanilla extract thoroughly in a sizable mixing dish.
- Mixing until smooth, gradually incorporate the dry ingredients into the wet ones.
- Add the chopped almonds, dark chocolate chips, and, if using, the shredded coconut.
- Using cupcake liners that have been prepared, divide the batter equally.
- When a toothpick put into the center comes out clean, bake for 20 to 25 minutes.
- After letting the cupcakes cool in the pan for five minutes, move them to a wire rack to finish cooling.

DIETARY GUIDELINES FOR DIABETES:
Compared to regular cupcakes, these have more healthy fats and fewer carbohydrates because they are baked with coconut oil and almond flour. Additionally, they have chopped almonds and shredded coconut, which give protein and fiber to help control blood sugar levels.

SHAPES AND BENEFITS:
Cupcakes are easy to portion control because they are convenient single servings. A rich and moist texture is provided by almond flour and coconut oil; chopped almonds and shredded coconut add texture and flavor reminiscent of the original Almond Joy candy bar.

Espresso Chocolate Cake

INGREDIENTS:
- All-purpose flour: 1 1/2 cups
- Baking powder: 1 teaspoon
- Baking soda: 1/2 teaspoon

- Salt: 1/4 teaspoon
- Unsweetened cocoa powder: 3/4 cup
- Granulated sugar or sweetener of choice: 1 cup
- Eggs: 2 large
- Milk or unsweetened almond milk: 1 cup
- Strong brewed coffee or espresso, cooled: 1/2 cup
- Vegetable oil: 1/2 cup
- Vanilla extract: 1 teaspoon

INSTRUCTIONS:
- Turn the oven on to 350°F (175°C), and dust a 9x13-inch baking pan with flour.
- Mix the flour, baking soda, baking powder, salt, and cocoa powder in a medium-sized bowl.
- Mix the sugar, eggs, milk, cooled coffee or espresso, vegetable oil, and vanilla extract thoroughly in a large mixing basin.
- Mixing until smooth, gradually incorporate the dry ingredients into the wet ones.
- Using a spatula, level the top of the batter once it has been poured into the baking pan.
- When a toothpick put into the center comes out clean, bake for 25 to 30 minutes.
- Let the cake set for ten minutes in the pan before slicing it into squares and serving.

DIETARY GUIDELINES FOR DIABETES:
Compared to regular chocolate cakes, this one has less sugar, and the addition of strong brewed coffee or espresso brings out the flavor of chocolate without adding more calories or sugar. Calcium and protein are added to milk or almond milk to help balance blood sugar levels.

SHAPES AND BENEFITS:
This cake bakes well when sliced into squares for simple serving after baking in a rectangular baking pan. Espresso and chocolate combine to create a flavor profile that is rich and decadent, ideal for coffee enthusiasts.

Pumpkin Spice Cake

INGREDIENTS:
- All-purpose flour: 1 1/2 cups
- Baking powder: 1 teaspoon
- Baking soda: 1/2 teaspoon
- Salt: 1/4 teaspoon
- Ground cinnamon: 1 teaspoon
- Ground ginger: 1/2 teaspoon
- Ground nutmeg: 1/4 teaspoon

- Ground cloves: 1/4 teaspoon
- Granulated sugar or sweetener of choice: 1 cup
- Eggs: 2 large
- Pumpkin puree: 1 cup
- Vegetable oil or melted coconut oil: 1/2 cup
- Milk or unsweetened almond milk: 1/4 cup
- Vanilla extract: 1 teaspoon

INSTRUCTIONS:
- Warm up the oven to 350°F (175°C) and dust a 9-inch circular cake pan with flour.
- Mix the flour, baking soda, baking powder, salt, nutmeg, cloves, cinnamon, and ginger in a medium-sized bowl.
- Mix the sugar, eggs, oil, milk, vanilla extract, and pureed pumpkin in a sizable mixing basin until thoroughly blended.
- Mixing until smooth, gradually incorporate the dry ingredients into the wet ones.
- Using a spatula, level the top of the batter after pouring it into the prepared cake pan.
- When a toothpick put into the center comes out clean, bake for 25 to 30 minutes.
- After letting the cake set in the pan for ten minutes, move it to a wire rack to finish cooling.

DIETARY GUIDELINES FOR DIABETES:
Compared to regular cakes, this one has less sugar and more vitamins, minerals, and fiber from the pureed pumpkin, all of which can help control blood sugar levels. The blend of spices enhances flavor without adding extra fat or calories.

SHAPES AND BENEFITS:
This cake, when baked in a circular cake pan, has a flavor profile that is warm and cozy and ideal for fall. Due to its high fiber content and low-calorie content, pumpkin is a healthy addition to desserts for those who have Diabetes.

Banana Walnut Cake with Greek Yogurt Frosting

INGREDIENTS:
- Ripe bananas, mashed: 2 cups
- Eggs: 2 large
- Granulated sugar or sweetener of choice: 1/2 cup
- Vegetable oil or melted coconut oil: 1/2 cup
- Vanilla extract: 1 teaspoon
- All-purpose flour: 1 1/2 cups
- Baking powder: 1 teaspoon

- Baking soda: 1/2 teaspoon
- Salt: 1/4 teaspoon
- Chopped walnuts: 1/2 cup
- Plain Greek yogurt: 1 cup
- Honey or maple syrup: 2 tablespoons

INSTRUCTIONS:
- Heat the oven to 350°F (175°C). Lightly coat a 9-by-9-inch square baking pan with flour and oil.
- Beat the eggs, sugar, oil, vanilla extract, and mashed bananas thoroughly in a sizable mixing basin.
- Sift the flour, baking soda, baking powder, and salt in a separate basin.
- Mix until just incorporated, and gradually add the dry ingredients to the wet ones.
- Add the chopped walnuts and fold.
- Using a spatula, level the top of the batter once it has been poured into the baking pan.
- When a toothpick put into the center comes out clean, bake for 25 to 30 minutes.
- After letting the cake set in the pan for ten minutes, move it to a wire rack to finish cooling.
- Combine the Greek yogurt and honey or maple syrup in a small bowl. After the cake has cooled, cover it with icing.

DIETARY GUIDELINES FOR DIABETES:
This cake has less added sugar than regular cakes because it is sweetened just with ripe bananas and a tiny bit of honey or maple syrup. Greek yogurt, which can help control blood sugar levels and promote digestive health, adds protein and probiotics to the frosting.

SHAPES AND BENEFITS:
Baked in a square baking pan, this cake has a crunchy walnut addition and is moist and tasty. Potassium and fiber, which are abundant in bananas, can lower blood pressure and improve digestive health.

Black Forest Cupcakes

INGREDIENTS:
- All-purpose flour: 1 1/2 cups
- Unsweetened cocoa powder: 1/2 cup
- Baking powder: 1 teaspoon
- Baking soda: 1/2 teaspoon
- Salt: 1/4 teaspoon
- Granulated sugar or sweetener of choice: 1 cup
- Eggs: 2 large
- Vegetable oil: 1/2 cup
- Milk or unsweetened almond milk: 1 cup

◇ Vanilla extract: 1 teaspoon
◇ Cherry pie filling (no sugar added): 1 cup
◇ Whipped cream or whipped coconut cream: for topping
◇ Fresh cherries (optional): for garnish

INSTRUCTIONS:
◇ Cake liners should be placed inside a muffin tray, and the oven should be preheated to 350°F/175°C.
◇ Combine the flour, baking soda, baking powder, cocoa powder, and salt in a medium-sized basin.
◇ Combine the sugar, eggs, milk, oil, and vanilla extract in a sizable mixing basin and whisk until thoroughly blended.
◇ Mix the dry ingredients until smooth, then gradually add them to the wet components.
◇ Equally distribute the batter into the lined cupcake liners, filling them approximately two-thirds of the way.
◇ Cook for eighteen to twenty minutes or until a toothpick inserted in the center comes out clean.
◇ After the cupcakes have cooled in the pan for five minutes, move them to a wire rack to finish cooling.
◇ After the cupcakes cool down, make a slight indent in the middle of each one with a knife. Pour the cherry pie filling into each well.
◇ Add a dollop of whipped cream or whipped coconut cream to the top of each cupcake, and garnish with a fresh cherry if you like.

NUTRITION PLAN FOR DIABETICS:
These cupcakes are lower in sugar compared to traditional Black Forest cakes, and the use of cherry pie filling with no added sugar reduces the overall sugar content. Cherries are relatively low on the glycemic index and contain antioxidants that may help improve insulin sensitivity.

SHAPES AND BENEFITS:
Cupcakes are convenient single servings, making portion control more accessible. The combination of chocolate cake, cherry filling, and whipped cream creates a decadent dessert reminiscent of the classic Black Forest cake.

Pineapple Coconut Cake

INGREDIENTS:
◇ All-purpose flour: 1 1/2 cups
◇ Baking powder: 1 teaspoon
◇ Baking soda: 1/2 teaspoon
◇ Salt: 1/4 teaspoon
◇ Granulated sugar or sweetener of choice: 3/4 cup
◇ Eggs: 2 large
◇ Vegetable oil or melted coconut oil: 1/2 cup

- ◇ Pineapple juice: 1/2 cup
- ◇ Vanilla extract: 1 teaspoon
- ◇ Crushed pineapple, drained: 1 cup
- ◇ Shredded coconut (unsweetened): 1/2 cup

INSTRUCTIONS:

- ◇ Warm up the oven to 350°F (175°C) and dust a 9-inch circular cake pan with flour.
- ◇ Mix the flour, baking soda, baking powder, and salt in a medium-sized bowl.
- ◇ Mix the sugar, eggs, oil, pineapple juice, and vanilla extract thoroughly in a sizable mixing basin.
- ◇ Mixing until smooth, gradually incorporate the dry ingredients into the wet ones.
- ◇ Stir in the chopped coconut and smashed pineapple.
- ◇ Using a spatula, level the top of the batter after pouring it into the prepared cake pan.
- ◇ When a toothpick put into the center comes out clean, bake for 25 to 30 minutes.
- ◇ After letting the cake set in the pan for ten minutes, move it to a wire rack to finish cooling.

DIETARY GUIDELINES FOR DIABETES:

Compared to classic pineapple coconut cakes, this cake has less added sugar, and the addition of crushed pineapple offers natural sweetness and fiber. Vitamin C and manganese, which can enhance immune system performance and bone health, are found in pineapples.

SHAPES AND BENEFITS:

This cake, which tastes great in the summer, is baked in a circular cake pan and has a tropical flavor profile. Pineapple and coconut give sweetness and texture, making this dessert tasty and moist—perfect for people with Diabetes.

Delicious Pies and Tarts

Sugar-Free Apple Pie

INGREDIENTS:
- Pie crust (prepared or homemade): 1 (9-inch)
- Apples, peeled, cored, and thinly sliced: 6 cups
- Lemon juice: 2 tablespoons
- Granulated sweetener of choice: 1/2 cup
- Ground cinnamon: 1 teaspoon
- Ground nutmeg: 1/4 teaspoon
- Cornstarch: 2 tablespoons
- Salt: 1/4 teaspoon

INSTRUCTIONS:
- Turn the oven on to 375°F, or 190°C.
- Toss apple slices with lemon juice in a big bowl.
- Combine the sweetener, nutmeg, cinnamon, cornstarch, and salt in another basin. Toss to coat after adding the apples.
- Fill pie crust with apple mixture. Cut slits on the top, seal the edges, and cover with the top crust.
- Bake for 50–60 minutes, or until the crust is golden brown and the apples are soft.
- Before serving, allow to cool.

DIETARY GUIDELINES FOR DIABETES:
People living with Diabetes can enjoy this apple pie because it has no added sugar and a low-carb crust. Apples offer natural sweetness and fiber, and the ingredients in the crust won't raise blood sugar levels.

SHAPES AND BENEFITS:
Taking the shape of a regular round pie, this delicacy provides all the comforts of traditional apple pie without the extra sugar.

Berry Almond Tart

INGREDIENTS:
- Almond flour: 1 1/2 cups
- Butter, melted: 1/4 cup
- Granulated sweetener of choice: 1/4 cup
- Salt: 1/4 teaspoon
- Mixed berries (strawberries, blueberries, raspberries): 2 cups
- Lemon juice: 2 tablespoons
- Granulated sweetener of choice: 2 tablespoons
- Almond extract: 1 teaspoon

INSTRUCTIONS:

- ◇ Set oven temperature to 175°C/350°F.
- ◇ Almond flour, melted butter, sweetener, and salt should all be combined in a bowl and crumbled. Fill tart pan with press.
- ◇ Berries should be combined with sweetener, almond extract, and lemon juice in a separate bowl. Place on top of crust.
- ◇ Bake for 25 to 30 minutes, or until the berries are bubbling and the crust is brown.
- ◇ Before serving, allow to cool.

DIETARY GUIDELINES FOR DIABETES:
Compared to standard crusts, almond flour has more healthful fats and fewer carbohydrates in this tart. Berries are a low-sugar, high-fiber, and antioxidant dessert that works well for people with Diabetes.

SHAPES AND BENEFITS:
Served on a nutty almond crust, this dessert has a gorgeous round tart shape that highlights the flavors and colors of a variety of berries.

Key Lime Pie with Almond Crust

INGREDIENTS:
- ◇ Almond flour: 1 1/2 cups
- ◇ Butter, melted: 1/4 cup
- ◇ Granulated sweetener of choice: 1/4 cup
- ◇ Salt: 1/4 teaspoon
- ◇ Lime zest: 2 tablespoons
- ◇ Lime juice: 1/2 cup
- ◇ Sweetened condensed milk (sugar-free if available): 14 ounces
- ◇ Eggs: 3, separated

INSTRUCTIONS:
- ◇ Set oven temperature to 175°C/350°F.
- ◇ Almond flour, melted butter, sweetener, salt, and one tablespoon of lime zest should all be combined in a bowl. Transfer to a pie plate.
- ◇ Bake for 10 minutes, then remove and allow to cool.
- ◇ Whisk together egg yolks, sweetened condensed milk, and lime juice in a separate bowl. Transfer to the chilled crust.
- ◇ Beat the egg whites in another dish until firm peaks form. Fold in the remaining lime zest gently.
- ◇ Meringue should be spread over pie filling, sealing sides tightly.
- ◇ Meringue should be baked for 15 minutes or until golden brown.
- ◇ Before serving, allow to cool.

DIETARY GUIDELINES FOR DIABETES:
This key lime pie has fewer carbohydrates since it has an almond crust rather than a typical pastry. The low sugar content is achieved by using sweetener and sugar-free sweetened condensed milk in place of sugar.

SHAPES AND BENEFITS:

This dessert, which has a traditional pie shape but a twist, is ideal for people seeking a lighter alternative because it combines the refreshing tang of key lime with a nutty almond crust.

Pumpkin Pie with Pecan Crust

INGREDIENTS:
- Pecans: 1 cup
- Almond flour: 1 cup
- Butter, melted: 1/4 cup
- Granulated sweetener of choice: 1/4 cup
- Salt: 1/4 teaspoon
- Pumpkin puree: 1 can (15 ounces)
- Eggs: 2
- Heavy cream: 1 cup
- Granulated sweetener of choice: 1/2 cup
- Pumpkin pie spice: 1 tablespoon
- Vanilla extract: 1 teaspoon

INSTRUCTIONS:
- Set oven temperature to 175°C/350°F.
- Pulse pecans in a food processor until finely ground. Add salt, sugar, melted butter, and almond flour. Blend until well blended.
- Form crust by pressing mixture into pie plate. After ten minutes of baking, allow to cool.
- Combine pumpkin puree, eggs, heavy cream, vanilla extract, sugar, and pumpkin pie spice in a bowl.
- Transfer filling to chilled crust.
- Bake the filling for 50–60 minutes or until it sets.
- Before serving, allow to cool.

DIETARY GUIDELINES FOR DIABETES:
Using a pecan crust instead of regular pastry gives this pumpkin pie a nutty flavor and lowers the amount of carbohydrates. The low sugar level is maintained by using heavy cream rather than milk and sugar-free sweeteners.

FORMS AND ADVANTAGES:
This dish, in the cozy shape of a round pie, is a lovely treat for fall celebrations because it mixes the warm aromas of pumpkin pie with the crunch of pecans.

Lemon Blueberry Tart

INGREDIENTS:
- Almond flour: 1 1/2 cups
- Butter, melted: 1/4 cup

- ◇ Granulated sweetener of choice: 1/4 cup
- ◇ Salt: 1/4 teaspoon
- ◇ Fresh blueberries: 2 cups
- ◇ Lemon juice: 1/4 cup
- ◇ Lemon zest: 2 tablespoons
- ◇ Granulated sweetener of choice: 1/4 cup
- ◇ Cornstarch: 2 tablespoons
- ◇ Eggs: 2

INSTRUCTIONS:
- ◇ Set oven temperature to 175°C/350°F.
- ◇ Pulse pecans in a food processor until finely ground. Add salt, sugar, melted butter, and almond flour. Blend until well blended.
- ◇ Form crust by pressing mixture into pie plate. After ten minutes of baking, allow to cool.
- ◇ Combine pumpkin puree, eggs, heavy cream, vanilla extract, sugar, and pumpkin pie spice in a bowl.
- ◇ Transfer filling to chilled crust.
- ◇ Bake the filling for 50–60 minutes or until it sets.
- ◇ Before serving, allow to cool.

DIETARY GUIDELINES FOR DIABETES:
Using a pecan crust instead of regular pastry gives this pumpkin pie a nutty flavor and lowers the amount of carbohydrates. The low sugar level is maintained by using heavy cream rather than milk and sugar-free sweeteners.

FORMS AND ADVANTAGES:
This dish, in the cozy shape of a round pie, is a lovely treat for fall celebrations because it mixes the warm aromas of pumpkin pie with the crunch of pecans.

Peach Raspberry Galette

INGREDIENTS:
- ◇ Pie crust (prepared or homemade): 1 (9-inch)
- ◇ Fresh peaches, sliced: 2 cups
- ◇ Fresh raspberries: 1 cup
- ◇ Granulated sweetener of choice: 1/4 cup
- ◇ Cornstarch: 1 tablespoon
- ◇ Lemon juice: 1 tablespoon
- ◇ Almond flour: 2 tablespoons
- ◇ Egg, beaten: 1
- ◇ Optional: Sliced almonds for topping

INSTRUCTIONS:
- ◇ Turn the oven on to 375°F, or 190°C.

◇ Peaches and raspberries should be combined with almond flour, cornstarch, lemon juice, and sweetener in a big basin.
◇ On a baking sheet covered with paper, roll out the pie crust.
◇ Leaving a border around the borders, spoon the fruit mixture into the center of the crust.
◇ Pinch the crust's edges together and fold them over the fruit, if necessary.
◇ Spread beaten egg over the crust and, if desired, top with chopped almonds.
◇ Bake for 30 to 35 minutes, or until the fruit is bubbling and the crust is brown.
◇ Before serving, allow to cool.

DIETARY GUIDELINES FOR DIABETES:
This low-sugar, high-fiber, antioxidant-rich galette is made with fresh peaches and raspberries in a basic pie crust. Almond flour lowers the carb count while adding a nutty flavor and texture to the filling.

SHAPES AND BENEFITS:
This galette's free-form, rustic design highlights the fruit filling's inherent sweetness and juiciness while being relatively simple to prepare.

Chocolate Pecan Pie Bars

INGREDIENTS:
◇ Almond flour: 1 1/2 cups
◇ Butter, melted: 1/4 cup
◇ Granulated sweetener of choice: 1/4 cup
◇ Salt: 1/4 teaspoon
◇ Pecans, chopped: 1 cup
◇ Sugar-free chocolate chips: 1/2 cup
◇ Eggs: 2
◇ Sugar-free maple syrup or sweetener of choice: 1/2 cup
◇ Vanilla extract: 1 teaspoon

INSTRUCTIONS:
◇ Set aside eight by 8 inches of parchment paper, leaving a little overhang on the sides for easy removal, and preheat the oven to 350°F (175°C).
◇ Combine almond flour, salt, sweetener, and melted butter in a bowl. Press onto the bottom of the baking pan that has been ready.
◇ Bake for ten minutes on the crust.
◇ In the meantime, combine chocolate chips and chopped pecans in a small bowl. Cover the partially baked crust with an equal layer.
◇ Whisk eggs, sugar-free maple syrup, and vanilla extract in a separate basin. Drizzle the layer of chocolate chips and pecans on top.
◇ Bake until the filling is firm, 25 to 30 minutes.
◇ Before cutting into bars, let the pan cool fully.

DIETARY GUIDELINES FOR DIABETES:

These bars have fewer carbohydrates because they are produced with almond flour and are sugar-free. Pecans are an excellent source of fiber and beneficial fats that can help control blood sugar levels.

SHAPES AND BENEFITS:
These sweets are perfect for on-the-go snacking because they are easy to portion out when cut into little bars. They have a rich chocolate flavor without any extra sugar and a gratifying crunch from the pecans.

Coconut Cream Pie

INGREDIENTS:
- Pie crust (prepared or homemade): 1 (9-inch)
- Coconut milk: 2 cups
- Unsweetened shredded coconut: 1 cup
- Eggs: 4, separated
- Granulated sweetener of choice: 1/2 cup
- Cornstarch: 1/4 cup
- Salt: 1/4 teaspoon
- Vanilla extract: 1 teaspoon

INSTRUCTIONS:
- Set oven temperature to 175°C/350°F.
- Bake pie crust in accordance with the recipe or instructions on the package. Allow to cool thoroughly.
- Steam the coconut milk and shredded coconut in a saucepan over medium heat, being careful not to boil. Take off the heat.
- Beat the egg yolks, sweetener, cornstarch, and salt together in a bowl until smooth.
- Stir in the heated coconut milk mixture gradually.
- Put the mixture back in the pot and whisk continuously over medium heat until it thickens.
- After taking off the heat, whisk in the vanilla essence. Allow to cool a little.
- Fill the chilled pie shell with the filling.
- Beat the egg whites in another dish until firm peaks form. Cover with pie filling.
- The meringue should bake for 15 to 20 minutes or until golden brown.
- Before serving, allow to cool.

DIETARY GUIDELINES FOR DIABETES:
Compared to regular dairy-based pies, this coconut cream pie has fewer carbs because it uses coconut milk and shredded coconut. The low sugar level is achieved in part by using almond flour in the crust and sugar-free sweeteners.

SHAPES AND BENEFITS:
Presented in a traditional round pie form, this dessert is a delicious treat for lovers of coconut. The fluffy meringue on top enhances its creamy richness.

Strawberry Rhubarb Crisp

INGREDIENTS:
- Rhubarb, chopped: 3 cups
- Strawberries, sliced: 2 cups
- Granulated sweetener of choice: 1/2 cup
- Lemon juice: 2 tablespoons
- Almond flour: 1 cup
- Rolled oats: 1 cup
- Granulated sweetener of choice: 1/2 cup
- Cinnamon: 1 teaspoon
- Butter, melted: 1/2 cup

INSTRUCTIONS:
- Set oven temperature to 175°C/350°F.
- Sweetener, lemon juice, sliced strawberries, and chopped rhubarb should all be combined in a bowl. Coat by tossing, then move to a baking dish that has been oiled.
- Combine cinnamon, sweetener, rolled oats, and almond flour in a separate bowl. Add melted butter and stir until crumbly.
- Cover the fruit in the baking dish with the crumble mixture.
- Bake for 30 to 35 minutes, until the topping is golden brown and the fruit is bubbling.
- Before serving, allow it to cool somewhat.

DIETARY GUIDELINES FOR DIABETES:
The fruit filling in this crisp has been sweetened using a low-calorie sweetener to lower its sugar level. Almond flour and oats are used to make the topping; these ingredients have fewer carbs than regular flour-based toppings.

SHAPES AND BENEFITS:
Topped with a crispy oat-almond topping, this crisp, baked in a rectangular baking dish, offers a comforting blend of tart rhubarb and sweet strawberries.

Mini Lemon Meringue Pies

INGREDIENTS:
- Pie crust (prepared or homemade): 12 mini tart shells
- Lemon juice: 1/2 cup
- Lemon zest: 2 tablespoons
- Granulated sweetener of choice: 1/2 cup
- Cornstarch: 2 tablespoons
- Water: 1 cup
- Egg yolks: 4
- Butter: 2 tablespoons
- Egg whites: 4

◇ Cream of tartar: 1/4 teaspoon
◇ Granulated sweetener of choice: 1/4 cup

INSTRUCTIONS:
◇ Set oven temperature to 175°C/350°F.
◇ Bake tart shells as directed on the package or in the recipe. Allow to cool thoroughly.
◇ Whisk the lemon juice, zest, cornstarch, sweetener, and water in a saucepan. Cook until thickened, about medium heat.
◇ Beat egg yolks with a fork. Pour the egg mixture back into the saucepan after gradually whisking in a little amount of the hot lemon mixture to temper the eggs. Cook, stirring regularly, for an additional two minutes.
◇ Take off the heat and mix in the melted butter. Allow to cool a little.
◇ Fill tart shells with chilled lemon filling.
◇ Beat the egg whites and cream of tartar in a sanitized bowl until soft peaks form. Add sweetener gradually while beating until stiff peaks form.
◇ Meringue can be piped or smeared over the lemon filling.
◇ Meringue should be baked for 10 to 12 minutes or until golden brown.
◇ Before serving, allow to cool.

DIABETIC NUTRITION PLAN:
Made with a sugar-free lemon filling and meringue topping, these small lemon meringue pies are low in sugar and portion-regulated. Using a low-carb crust or almond flour helps reduce the amount of carbohydrates.

SHAPES AND BENEFITS:
Baked in tiny tart shells, these pies are the ideal individual-sized dessert choice because of their delicious blend of fluffy meringue and tart lemon filling.

Mixed Berry Galette

INGREDIENTS:
◇ Pie crust (prepared or homemade): 1 (9-inch)
◇ Mixed berries (strawberries, blueberries, raspberries): 3 cups
◇ Granulated sweetener of choice: 1/4 cup
◇ Cornstarch: 2 tablespoons
◇ Lemon juice: 2 tablespoons
◇ Egg, beaten: 1

INSTRUCTIONS:
◇ Turn the oven on to 375°F, or 190°C.
◇ On a baking sheet covered with paper, roll out the pie crust.
◇ Combine the mixed berries, cornstarch, sweetener, and lemon juice in a bowl. Leaving a border around the edges, spoon the mixture onto the center of the crust.
◇ Pinch the crust's edges together and fold them over the fruit, if necessary.
◇ Use the beaten egg to brush the crust.

- ♡ Bake for 30 to 35 minutes, or until the fruit is bubbling and the crust is brown.
- ♡ Before serving, allow to cool.

DIETARY GUIDELINES FOR DIABETES:
This is a low-sugar, high-fiber, antioxidant-packed galette made using a basic pie crust filled with a mixture of berries. Using a low-carb crust or almond flour helps reduce the amount of carbohydrates.

BENEFITS AND SHAPES:
This galette's free-form, rustic design highlights the natural sweetness and juiciness of the mixed berries while being relatively simple to make.

Almond Flour Apple Tart

INGREDIENTS:
- ♡ Almond flour: 1 1/2 cups
- ♡ Butter, melted: 1/4 cup
- ♡ Granulated sweetener of choice: 1/4 cup
- ♡ Salt: 1/4 teaspoon
- ♡ Apples, thinly sliced: 3 cups
- ♡ Lemon juice: 2 tablespoons
- ♡ Granulated sweetener of choice: 1/4 cup
- ♡ Cinnamon: 1 teaspoon
- ♡ Almond slices: for topping

INSTRUCTIONS:
- ♡ Set oven temperature to 175°C/350°F.
- ♡ Combine almond flour, salt, sweetener, and melted butter in a bowl. Fill tart pan with press.
- ♡ Bake for 10 minutes, then remove and allow to cool.
- ♡ Apple slices should be combined with cinnamon, sugar, and lemon juice in a separate bowl. Place on top of crust.
- ♡ Almond slices should be sprinkled on top.
- ♡ Bake for 25 to 30 minutes, or until the crust is golden brown and the apples are soft.
- ♡ Before serving, allow to cool.

DIETARY GUIDELINES FOR DIABETES:
Almond flour is used in place of regular dough in this apple dessert, which lowers the amount of carbohydrates. Apples are a healthy choice for people with Diabetes since they are high in fiber and low in sugar.

SHAPES AND BENEFITS:
This dish, baked in a round tart pan, is a soothing and fulfilling treat that combines the traditional flavors of apples and cinnamon with a nutty almond crust.

Cherry Almond Crumble

INGREDIENTS:
- Cherry pie filling (no sugar added): 1 can (21 ounces)
- Almond flour: 1 cup
- Rolled oats: 1 cup
- Granulated sweetener of choice: 1/4 cup
- Butter, melted: 1/2 cup
- Almond slices: for topping

INSTRUCTIONS:
- Set oven temperature to 175°C/350°F.
- Pour the cherry pie filling into the bottom of a baking dish that has been oiled.
- Crumble together almond flour, melted butter, rolled oats, and sweetener in a bowl.
- Evenly scatter the crumble mixture over the cherry filling.
- Add slices of almond on top.
- Bake for 30 to 35 minutes, or until the mixture is bubbling and the topping is golden brown.
- Before serving, allow it to cool somewhat.

DIETARY GUIDELINES FOR DIABETES:
This low-calorie sweetened fruit filling lowers the amount of sugar in the cherry almond crumble. Almond flour and oats are used to make the topping; these ingredients have fewer carbs than regular flour-based toppings.

SHAPES AND BENEFITS:
Baked in a rectangular baking dish, this crumble is the ideal comfortable treat because it has a warming blend of sweet cherries and almond-flavored topping.

Maple Walnut Pie

INGREDIENTS:
- Pie crust (prepared or homemade): 1 (9-inch)
- Walnuts, chopped: 2 cups
- Granulated sweetener of choice: 1/2 cup
- Eggs: 3
- Sugar-free maple syrup: 1 cup
- Butter, melted: 1/4 cup
- Vanilla extract: 1 teaspoon

INSTRUCTIONS:
- Set oven temperature to 175°C/350°F.
- Bake pie crust in accordance with the recipe or instructions on the package. Allow to cool thoroughly.

- ◇ Combine the chopped walnuts, sweetener, eggs, melted butter, sugar-free maple syrup, and vanilla essence in a bowl and stir until thoroughly mixed.
- ◇ Spoon contents into pie shell after cooling.
- ◇ Bake the filling for 40 to 45 minutes or until it sets.
- ◇ Before serving, allow to cool.

DIETARY GUIDELINES FOR DIABETES:
The sugar and carbohydrate content of this maple walnut pie is decreased by using sugar-free maple syrup and a low-carb crust. An excellent source of protein and healthful fats, walnuts can help control blood sugar levels.

FORMS AND ADVANTAGES:
With its traditional round pie form, its rich maple syrup flavor, and crunchy walnuts, this dessert is a delightful treat that goes well with any meal.

Chocolate Silk Tart

INGREDIENTS:
- ◇ Almond flour: 1 1/2 cups
- ◇ Butter, melted: 1/4 cup
- ◇ Granulated sweetener of choice: 1/4 cup
- ◇ Salt: 1/4 teaspoon
- ◇ Sugar-free chocolate chips: 1 cup
- ◇ Heavy cream: 1 cup
- ◇ Eggs: 3
- ◇ Granulated sweetener of choice: 1/4 cup
- ◇ Vanilla extract: 1 teaspoon

INSTRUCTIONS:
- ◇ Preheat oven to 350°F (175°C).
- ◇ In a bowl, mix almond flour, melted butter, sweetener, and salt. Press into the tart pan.
- ◇ Bake the crust for 10 minutes, then let it cool.
- ◇ In a saucepan, melt chocolate chips and heavy cream over low heat, stirring until smooth. Remove from heat and let cool slightly.
- ◇ In a separate bowl, whisk eggs, sweetener, and vanilla extract until well combined.
- ◇ Gradually whisk the chocolate mixture into the egg mixture until smooth.
- ◇ Pour filling into cooled crust.
- ◇ Bake for 25-30 minutes, until filling is set.
- ◇ Let cool before serving.

NUTRITION PLAN FOR DIABETICS:
This chocolate silk tart uses almond flour instead of traditional pastry, reducing the carbohydrate content. The use of sugar-free chocolate chips and sweeteners helps keep the sugar content low.

SHAPES AND BENEFITS:

Baked in a round tart pan, this dessert offers a silky smooth chocolate filling atop a nutty almond crust, making it a decadent yet diabetic-friendly treat.

Indulgent Cookies and Bars

Oatmeal Raisin Cookies

INGREDIENTS:
- Rolled oats: 2 cups
- Almond flour: 1 cup
- Baking powder: 1 teaspoon
- Cinnamon: 1 teaspoon
- Salt: 1/4 teaspoon
- Butter, softened: 1/2 cup
- Granulated sweetener of choice: 1/2 cup
- Eggs: 2
- Vanilla extract: 1 teaspoon
- Raisins: 1 cup

INSTRUCTIONS:
- Adjust the oven temperature to 350°F (175°C) and place parchment paper on a baking pan.
- Combine almond flour, baking powder, cinnamon, salt, and rolled oats in a bowl.
- Beat sweetener and softened butter together in a separate dish until smooth. Beat in the vanilla essence and eggs thoroughly.
- Mixing until mixed, gradually add the dry ingredients to the wet ones.
- Add the raisins and stir.
- Drop dough by spoonfuls, spacing them apart, onto the baking sheet that has been prepared.
- Using the back of a spoon, slightly flatten each cookie.
- Bake for ten to twelve minutes or until well browned.
- After cooling the baking sheet for a few minutes, move the baked goods to a wire rack to finish cooling.

DIETARY GUIDELINES FOR DIABETES:
Almond flour and an alternative sugar are used to make these oatmeal raisin cookies, which lowers their carbohydrate load. Fiber from oats has the potential to help control blood sugar levels.

SHAPES AND BENEFITS:
Traditional round cookies with the comforting aromas of raisins and oats, these candies are ideal as a satisfying dessert or as a snack.

Peanut Butter Chocolate Chip Bars

INGREDIENTS:
- Peanut butter, creamy: 1 cup
- Butter, melted: 1/2 cup
- Granulated sweetener of choice: 1 cup

- Eggs: 2
- Vanilla extract: 1 teaspoon
- Almond flour: 2 cups
- Baking powder: 1 teaspoon
- Salt: 1/4 teaspoon
- Sugar-free chocolate chips: 1 cup

INSTRUCTIONS:
- Warm up the oven to 350°F (175°C) and coat a 9-by-13-inch baking dish with oil.
- Combine peanut butter, melted butter, eggs, sugar, and vanilla extract in a big bowl and stir until well combined.
- Add the baking powder, salt, and almond flour and stir until well blended.
- Add sugar-free chocolate chips and stir.
- Pour the batter into the baking pan that has been prepared evenly.
- A toothpick put into the center should come out clean after 20 to 25 minutes of baking or until the edges are golden brown.
- Allow the pan to cool fully before slicing into bars.

DIETARY GUIDELINES FOR DIABETES:
Almond flour and a sugar alternative are used to make these peanut butter chocolate chip bars, which lowers the amount of carbohydrates. Protein and good fats found in peanut butter can help control blood sugar levels.

SHAPES AND BENEFITS:
These delights mix the rich flavors of chocolate chips and peanut butter, giving them a delightful and decadent snack when cut into rectangular bars.

Almond Flour Shortbread Cookies

INGREDIENTS:
- Almond flour: 2 cups
- Butter, softened: 1/2 cup
- Granulated sweetener of choice: 1/2 cup
- Vanilla extract: 1 teaspoon
- Salt: 1/4 teaspoon

INSTRUCTIONS:
- Adjust the oven temperature to 325°F (160°C) and place parchment paper on a baking pan.
- Beat softened butter, sweetener, vanilla extract, and salt together in a bowl until smooth.
- Add the almond flour to the butter mixture little by little and stir until a dough forms.
- After forming the dough into a log, cover it with plastic wrap. Place in the fridge to chill for a minimum of half an hour.
- After the dough has chilled, cut it into rounds and arrange them on the ready baking sheet.

◇ Bake until the edges are golden brown, 12 to 15 minutes.
◇ After cooling the baking sheet for a few minutes, move the baked goods to a wire rack to finish cooling.

DIETARY GUIDELINES FOR DIABETES:
The amount of carbohydrates in these shortbread cookies made with almond flour is decreased by using a sugar alternative. Protein and good fats found in almond flour can help control blood sugar levels.

SHAPES AND BENEFITS:
Traditionally shaped like rounds, these shortbread cookies have a buttery, crumbly texture and a hint of almond flavor. They go well with tea or coffee.

Chocolate Walnut Brownies

INGREDIENTS:
◇ Almond flour: 1 cup 120g *use plain if not*
◇ Cocoa powder: 1/2 cup 60g
◇ Baking powder: 1 teaspoon
◇ Salt: 1/4 teaspoon
◇ Butter, melted: 1/2 cup 120g
◇ Granulated sweetener of choice: 1 cup 200g
◇ Eggs: 3
◇ Vanilla extract: 1 teaspoon
◇ Chopped walnuts: 1/2 cup 75g

INSTRUCTIONS:
◇ Heat the oven to 350°F (175°C) and coat an 8-by-8-inch baking dish with oil.
◇ Mix the almond flour, baking powder, cocoa powder, and salt in a bowl.
◇ Melted butter, sweetener, eggs, and vanilla extract should all be combined smoothly in a separate basin.
◇ Mixing until thoroughly blended, gradually adding the dry ingredients to the wet components.
◇ Add the chopped walnuts and fold.
◇ Evenly distribute the batter after pouring it into the baking pan.
◇ When a toothpick is pushed into the center, a few moist crumbs should come out. Bake for 20 to 25 minutes.
◇ Allow the pan to cool fully before slicing into squares.

DIETARY GUIDELINES FOR DIABETES:
Almond flour and sugar substitutes are used to make these chocolate walnut brownies, which lowers their carbohydrate load. Protein and heart-healthy fats included in walnuts can help control blood sugar levels.

SHAPES AND BENEFITS:
These brownies are a delectable treat for chocolate fans, thick, fudgy, and full of chocolate flavor when cut into square pieces.

Cranberry Orange Biscotti

INGREDIENTS:
- Almond flour: 2 cups
- Granulated sweetener of choice: 1/2 cup
- Baking powder: 1 teaspoon
- Salt: 1/4 teaspoon
- Eggs: 2
- Vanilla extract: 1 teaspoon
- Orange zest: 2 tablespoons
- Dried cranberries: 1/2 cup
- Sliced almonds: 1/2 cup

INSTRUCTIONS:
- Adjust the oven temperature to 350°F (175°C) and place parchment paper on a baking pan.
- Mix the almond flour, baking powder, sweetener, and salt in a bowl.
- Beat eggs, orange zest, and vanilla essence thoroughly in a separate basin.
- Mix until dough forms, gradually adding the dry ingredients to the wet ones.
- Stir in sliced almonds and dried cranberries.
- On the baking sheet that has been prepared, form the dough into two logs.
- Bake until firm and gently golden, 25 to 30 minutes.
- After 10 minutes of cooling on the baking sheet, move to a chopping board.
- Using a serrated knife, cut the logs into diagonal pieces.
- Reposition the biscotti on the baking sheet and continue baking for a further 10 to 12 minutes or until they become crisp.
- Before serving, allow it to cool fully.

DIETARY GUIDELINES FOR DIABETES:
Almond flour and a sugar alternative are used to make these cranberry orange biscotti, which lowers the amount of carbohydrates. Almonds supply protein and good fats, while cranberries add tartness and antioxidants.

SHAPES AND BENEFITS:
The crunchy texture of these twice-baked biscotti goes well with tea or coffee. They are a lovely treat because of the tart cranberries and zesty orange peel combo.

Maple Pecan Bars

INGREDIENTS:
- Almond flour: 1 1/2 cups
- Granulated sweetener of choice: 1/2 cup

◇ Butter, melted: 1/2 cup
◇ Maple extract: 1 teaspoon
◇ Pecans, chopped: 1 cup

INSTRUCTIONS:
◇ Preheat the oven to 350°F (175°C), and place parchment paper inside an eight by 8-inch baking pan.
◇ Combine the melted butter, almond flour, sweetener, and maple extract in a bowl and stir until a dough forms.
◇ Fill the baking pan with dough, pressing it firmly.
◇ Evenly distribute chopped pecans over the dough, gently pushing them to the surface.
◇ Bake for twenty to twenty-five minutes or until the sides are browned.
◇ Allow the pan to cool fully before slicing into bars.

DIETARY GUIDELINES FOR DIABETES:
Almond flour and an alternative sugar are used to make these maple pecan treats, which lowers their carbohydrate load. Protein and good fats included in pecans can help control blood sugar levels.

SHAPES AND BENEFITS:
Sliced into rectangular bars, these sweets are an excellent alternative for a snack or dessert because they have a rich maple flavor and crunchy pecans.

Coconut Macaroons

INGREDIENTS:
◇ Unsweetened shredded coconut: 3 cups
◇ Granulated sweetener of choice: 1/2 cup
◇ Egg whites: 4
◇ Vanilla extract: 1 teaspoon
◇ Salt: 1/4 teaspoon

INSTRUCTIONS:
◇ Adjust the oven temperature to 325°F (160°C) and place parchment paper on a baking pan.
◇ Combine the shredded coconut, sweetener, vanilla essence, and salt in a bowl.
◇ Beat the egg whites in another dish until firm peaks form.
◇ Till they are thoroughly blended, gently fold the beaten egg whites into the coconut mixture.
◇ Spoon mixture onto a baking sheet that has been prepared; space them apart.
◇ Bake for twenty to twenty-five minutes or until browned.
◇ After cooling the baking sheet for a few minutes, move the baked goods to a wire rack to finish cooling.

DIETARY GUIDELINES FOR DIABETES:

The amount of carbohydrates in these coconut macaroons is decreased by using unsweetened shredded coconut and a sugar substitute. Protein, which is included in egg whites, helps to balance blood sugar levels.

SHAPES AND BENEFITS:
A delicious treat for coconut fans, these macaroons have a chewy texture and a sweet coconut flavor.

Espresso Chocolate Chunk Cookies

INGREDIENTS:
- Almond flour: 2 cups
- Cocoa powder: 1/4 cup
- Baking powder: 1 teaspoon
- Salt: 1/4 teaspoon
- Granulated sweetener of choice: 1/2 cup
- Butter, softened: 1/2 cup
- Espresso powder: 1 tablespoon
- Vanilla extract: 1 teaspoon
- Eggs: 2
- Sugar-free chocolate chunks: 1 cup

INSTRUCTIONS:
- Adjust the oven temperature to 350°F (175°C) and place parchment paper on a baking pan.
- Almond flour, cocoa powder, baking powder, salt, and espresso powder should all be combined in a basin.
- Beat sugar, vanilla extract, and softened butter together until smooth in a separate dish.
- One egg at a time, add them to the butter mixture, mixing thoroughly after each addition.
- Mixing until thoroughly blended, gradually adding the dry ingredients to the wet components.
- Stir in chocolate chunks without added sugar.
- Drop dough by spoonfuls, spacing them apart, onto the baking sheet that has been prepared.
- Using the back of a spoon, slightly flatten each cookie.
- Bake until the edges are firm, 10 to 12 minutes.
- After cooling the baking sheet for a few minutes, move the baked goods to a wire rack to finish cooling.

DIETARY GUIDELINES FOR DIABETES:
Almond flour and an alternative sugar are used to make these espresso chocolate chunk cookies, which lowers their carbohydrate load. Rich coffee flavor is added with espresso powder without using additional sugar.

SHAPES AND BENEFITS:
Traditionally shaped like rounds, these cookies have a rich chocolate and espresso flavor combination that makes them the ideal midday snack.

Lemon Poppy Seed Bars

INGREDIENTS:
- Almond flour: 2 cups
- Granulated sweetener of choice: 1/2 cup
- Baking powder: 1 teaspoon
- Salt: 1/4 teaspoon
- Poppy seeds: 2 tablespoons
- Butter, melted: 1/2 cup
- Lemon zest: 2 tablespoons
- Lemon juice: 1/4 cup
- Eggs: 2
- Vanilla extract: 1 teaspoon

INSTRUCTIONS:
- Heat the oven to 350°F (175°C) and coat an 8-by-8-inch baking dish with oil.
- Almond flour, sweetener, baking powder, salt, and poppy seeds should all be combined in a bowl.
- Melted butter, lemon zest, lemon juice, eggs, and vanilla essence should all be thoroughly mixed in a separate bowl.
- Mix until batter forms, gradually adding the dry components to the wet ones.
- Pour the batter into the baking pan that has been prepared evenly.
- A toothpick put into the center should come out clean after 20 to 25 minutes of baking or until the edges are golden brown.
- Allow the pan to cool fully before slicing into bars.

DIETARY GUIDELINES FOR DIABETES:
Almond flour and a sugar alternative are used to make these lemon poppy seed bars, which lowers their carbohydrate load. Zest and juice from lemons offer a zesty flavor without requiring any sugar.

SHAPES AND BENEFITS:
Sliced into rectangular bars, these sweet treats are the ideal choice for a snack or dessert because they have a crisp poppy seed texture and a pleasant lemon flavor.

Ginger Molasses Cookies

INGREDIENTS:
- Almond flour: 2 cups
- Granulated sweetener of choice: 1/2 cup
- Baking soda: 1 teaspoon
- Ground ginger: 1 tablespoon
- Ground cinnamon: 1 teaspoon

- ◇ Ground cloves: 1/2 teaspoon
- ◇ Salt: 1/4 teaspoon
- ◇ Butter, melted: 1/2 cup
- ◇ Molasses: 1/4 cup
- ◇ Egg: 1
- ◇ Vanilla extract: 1 teaspoon

INSTRUCTIONS:

◇ Adjust the oven temperature to 350°F (175°C) and place parchment paper on a baking pan.

◇ Mix the almond flour, baking soda, sweetener, ground ginger, ground cinnamon, ground cloves, and salt in a bowl.

◇ Melted butter, molasses, egg, and vanilla extract should all be thoroughly mixed in a separate basin.

◇ Mix until dough forms, gradually adding the dry ingredients to the wet ones.

◇ Form the dough into balls and arrange, spacing them apart, on the baking sheet that has been prepared.

◇ Using the back of a spoon, slightly flatten each cookie.

◇ Bake until the edges are firm, 10 to 12 minutes.

◇ After cooling the baking sheet for a few minutes, move the baked goods to a wire rack to finish cooling.

DIETARY GUIDELINES FOR DIABETES:

Almond flour and an alternative sugar are used to make these ginger molasses cookies, which lowers their carbohydrate load. Molasses add a rich flavor without using additional sugar.

SHAPES AND BENEFITS:

Traditionally shaped like rounds, these cookies have a warm, spicy flavor from the ginger, cinnamon, and cloves, which makes them a satisfying snack.

Pistachio Cranberry Biscotti

INGREDIENTS:

- ◇ Almond flour: 2 cups
- ◇ Granulated sweetener of choice: 1/2 cup
- ◇ Baking powder: 1 teaspoon
- ◇ Salt: 1/4 teaspoon
- ◇ Eggs: 2
- ◇ Vanilla extract: 1 teaspoon
- ◇ Pistachios, chopped: 1/2 cup
- ◇ Dried cranberries: 1/2 cup

INSTRUCTIONS:

◇ Adjust the oven temperature to 350°F (175°C) and place parchment paper on a baking pan.

- Mix the almond flour, baking powder, sweetener, and salt in a bowl.
- Beat eggs and vanilla extract thoroughly in a separate basin.
- Mix until a dough forms, and gradually add the dry ingredients to the egg mixture.
- Stir in the dried cranberries and chopped pistachios.
- On the baking sheet that has been prepared, form the dough into two logs.
- Bake until firm and gently golden, 20 to 25 minutes.
- After 10 minutes of cooling on the baking sheet, move to a chopping board.
- Using a serrated knife, cut the logs into diagonal pieces.
- Reposition the biscotti on the baking sheet and continue baking for a further 10 to 12 minutes or until they become crisp.
- Before serving, allow it to cool fully.

DIETARY GUIDELINES FOR DIABETES:
Almond flour and an alternative sugar are used to make these pistachio cranberry biscotti, which lowers their carbohydrate level. Cranberries and pistachios offer taste and texture without adding additional sugar.

SHAPES AND BENEFITS:
The crunchy texture of these twice-baked biscotti goes well with tea or coffee. The delicious contrast of flavors and hues is created when pistachios and cranberries are combined.

Chocolate Hazelnut Biscotti

INGREDIENTS:
- Almond flour: 2 cups
- Cocoa powder: 1/4 cup
- Granulated sweetener of choice: 1/2 cup
- Baking powder: 1 teaspoon
- Salt: 1/4 teaspoon
- Eggs: 2
- Vanilla extract: 1 teaspoon
- Hazelnuts, chopped: 1/2 cup
- Sugar-free chocolate chips: 1/2 cup

INSTRUCTIONS:
- Adjust the oven temperature to 350°F (175°C) and place parchment paper on a baking pan.
- Almond flour, baking powder, sweetener, cocoa powder, and salt should all be combined in a bowl.
- Beat eggs and vanilla extract thoroughly in a separate basin.
- Mix until a dough forms, and gradually add the dry ingredients to the egg mixture.
- Add the sugar-free chocolate chips and chopped hazelnuts and stir.

◇ On the baking sheet that has been prepared, form the dough into two logs.
◇ Bake until firm and gently golden, 20 to 25 minutes.
◇ After 10 minutes of cooling on the baking sheet, move to a chopping board.
◇ Using a serrated knife, cut the logs into diagonal pieces.
◇ Reposition the biscotti on the baking sheet and continue baking for a further 10 to 12 minutes or until they become crisp.
◇ Before serving, allow it to cool fully.

DIETARY GUIDELINES FOR DIABETES:
Almond flour and an alternative sugar are used to make these chocolate hazelnut biscotti, which lowers their carbohydrate level. Protein and good fats included in hazelnuts can help control blood sugar levels.

SHAPES AND BENEFITS:
The crunchy texture of these twice-baked biscotti goes well with tea or coffee. They are a rich delicacy because of the combination of toasted hazelnuts and rich chocolate.

Blueberry Oatmeal Bars

INGREDIENTS:
◇ Rolled oats: 2 cups
◇ Almond flour: 1 cup
◇ Baking powder: 1 teaspoon
◇ Cinnamon: 1 teaspoon
◇ Salt: 1/4 teaspoon
◇ Butter, melted: 1/2 cup
◇ Granulated sweetener of choice: 1/2 cup
◇ Eggs: 2
◇ Vanilla extract: 1 teaspoon
◇ Fresh blueberries: 1 1/2 cups

INSTRUCTIONS:
◇ Heat the oven to 350°F (175°C) and coat an 8-by-8-inch baking dish with oil.
◇ Combine almond flour, baking powder, cinnamon, salt, and rolled oats in a bowl.
◇ Beat sweetener, eggs, vanilla extract, and melted butter until smooth in a separate dish.
◇ Mixing until mixed, gradually add the dry ingredients to the wet ones.
◇ Add the fresh blueberries and fold.
◇ Pour the batter into the baking pan that has been prepared evenly.
◇ Bake for 25 to 30 minutes or until firm and golden brown.
◇ Allow the pan to cool fully before slicing into bars.

DIETARY GUIDELINES FOR DIABETES:

Almond flour and a sugar alternative are used to make these blueberry oatmeal bars, which lowers the amount of carbohydrates. Oats offer fiber to help control blood sugar levels, and blueberries add natural sweetness and antioxidants.

SHAPES AND BENEFITS:
Sliced into bars, these delights are a tasty and nutritious snack or dessert choice since they blend the wholesome goodness of oats with fresh blueberries.

Pumpkin Chocolate Chip Cookies

INGREDIENTS:
- Almond flour: 2 cups
- Pumpkin puree: 1/2 cup
- Granulated sweetener of choice: 1/2 cup
- Butter, softened: 1/2 cup
- Eggs: 2
- Vanilla extract: 1 teaspoon
- Pumpkin pie spice: 1 teaspoon
- Baking powder: 1 teaspoon
- Salt: 1/4 teaspoon
- Sugar-free chocolate chips: 1 cup

INSTRUCTIONS:
- Adjust the oven temperature to 350°F (175°C) and place parchment paper on a baking pan.
- Mix the almond flour, baking powder, pumpkin pie spice, and salt in a bowl.
- Beat softened butter, sugars, eggs, pureed pumpkin, and vanilla extract until smooth in a separate bowl.
- Mixing until mixed, gradually add the dry ingredients to the wet ones.
- Add sugar-free chocolate chips and stir.
- Drop dough by spoonfuls, spacing them apart, onto the baking sheet that has been prepared.
- Using the back of a spoon, slightly flatten each cookie.
- Bake until the edges are firm, 10 to 12 minutes.
- After cooling the baking sheet for a few minutes, move the baked goods to a wire rack to finish cooling.

DIETARY GUIDELINES FOR DIABETES:
Almond flour and an alternative sugar are used to make these pumpkin chocolate chip cookies, which lowers their carbohydrate load. Pumpkin pie spice lends a cozy, toasty flavor, and pumpkin puree adds moisture and fiber.

SHAPES AND BENEFITS:
Traditional round cookies are a delicious fall-inspired snack that perfectly balances chocolate chips and pumpkin flavor.

Apricot Almond Bars

INGREDIENTS:
- Almond flour: 1 1/2 cups
- Granulated sweetener of choice: 1/2 cup
- Baking powder: 1 teaspoon
- Salt: 1/4 teaspoon
- Butter, melted: 1/2 cup
- Almond extract: 1 teaspoon
- Eggs: 2
- Dried apricots, chopped: 1 cup
- Sliced almonds: 1/2 cup

INSTRUCTIONS:
- Heat the oven to 350°F (175°C) and coat an 8-by-8-inch baking dish with oil.
- Mix the almond flour, baking powder, sweetener, and salt in a bowl.
- Melted butter, almond essence, and eggs should be thoroughly mixed in a separate basin.
- Mixing until mixed, gradually add the dry ingredients to the wet ones.
- Add the sliced almonds and chopped dry apricots.
- Pour the batter into the baking pan that has been prepared evenly.
- Bake for 20 to 25 minutes or until firm and golden brown.
- Allow the pan to cool fully before slicing into bars.

DIETARY GUIDELINES FOR DIABETES:
Almond flour and a sugar replacement are used to make these apricot almond bars, which lowers the amount of carbohydrates. Almonds supply protein and good fats, and dried apricots add natural sweetness and fiber.

SHAPES AND BENEFITS:
Sliced into bars, the sweetness and tartness of dried apricots are paired with the crunch of sliced almonds to provide a delightful and wholesome snack or dessert choice.

Frozen Treats and Popsicles

Strawberry Greek Yogurt Popsicles

INGREDIENTS:
- Greek yogurt: 2 cups
- Fresh strawberries, chopped: 1 cup
- Granulated sweetener of choice: 2-3 tablespoons (optional)
- Vanilla extract: 1 teaspoon (optional)

INSTRUCTIONS:
- Greek yogurt, cut strawberries, sugar (if using), and vanilla extract (if using) should all be combined in a blender. Process till smooth.
- Leaving a small amount of space at the top for expansion, pour the mixture into the popsicle molds.
- Place the popsicle sticks into the molds, then freeze for four hours or until the popsicles are solid.
- After they have frozen, run the popsicles under some warm water for a little period to extract them from the molds.
- Serve right away or store in an airtight jar in the freezer.

DIETARY GUIDELINES FOR DIABETES:
Greek yogurt, which has fewer carbs and more protein than regular ice cream, is used to make these popsicles. Because fresh strawberries naturally include sweetness and fiber, there is less extra sugar when a sugar replacement is used.

SHAPES AND BENEFITS:
Enjoyable guilt-free, these popsicles are a creamy, refreshing pleasure. They are simple to prepare and a great way to cool yourself on warm days.

Avocado Lime Sorbet

INGREDIENTS:
- Ripe avocados, peeled and pitted: 2
- Fresh lime juice: 1/4 cup
- Granulated sweetener of choice: 1/4 cup
- Water: 1/2 cup

INSTRUCTIONS:
- Put the pitted and peeled avocados, water, sugar, and fresh lime juice in a blender.
- Blend until creamy and smooth, stopping the blender if needed to scrape down the edges.
- If desired, add extra sweetener after tasting the mixture to adjust the sweetness.

- ◇ Once the mixture is in a shallow dish, freeze it for four to six hours or until it solidifies.
- ◇ After the sorbet has frozen, scoop it into cones or serving bowls and serve right away.

DIETARY GUIDELINES FOR DIABETES:
Avocados, which are rich in nutrients and high in fiber and healthy fats, are used to make this sorbet. Lime juice gives a zesty, refreshing taste, and using a sugar alternative reduces the amount of added sugar.

SHAPES AND BENEFITS:
For individuals who are in the mood for something refreshing, avocado lime sorbet is a creamy, zesty dessert alternative. It gives a delicious sweetness without raising blood sugar levels, and it's simple to create.

Chocolate Banana Nice Cream

INGREDIENTS:
- ◇ Ripe bananas, peeled and sliced: 4
- ◇ Unsweetened cocoa powder: 2 tablespoons
- ◇ Vanilla extract: 1 teaspoon
- ◇ Almond milk (or any milk of choice): 1/4 cup
- ◇ Granulated sweetener of choice: 2-3 tablespoons (optional)

INSTRUCTIONS:
- ◇ Arrange the banana slices in a single layer on a parchment paper-lined baking sheet.
- ◇ The bananas should be frozen for at least two hours or until they are excellent.
- ◇ After freezing, move the bananas to a food processor or blender.
- ◇ Blend in the almond milk, cocoa powder, vanilla extract, and sweetener if using.
- ◇ Blend until creamy and smooth, stopping the blender if needed to scrape down the edges.
- ◇ If desired, add more sweetener after tasting the excellent cream to change the sweetness.
- ◇ For a firmer texture, transfer to a container and freeze, or serve immediately as a soft serve.

DIABETIC NUTRITION PLAN:
Frozen bananas add natural sweetness and fiber to this delicious cream. Rich chocolate flavor can be added without adding more sugar by using unsweetened cocoa powder and using a sugar substitute, which lowers the amount of additional sugar.

SHAPES AND BENEFITS:
A guilt-free, creamy texture and rich chocolate flavor characterize chocolate banana lovely cream, a healthier take on ice cream. It's simple to prepare and can be personalized by adding extras like berries or almonds as toppings.

Mango Coconut Ice Pops

INGREDIENTS:
- Ripe mangoes, peeled and diced: 2 cups
- Coconut milk: 1 cup
- Granulated sweetener of choice: 2-3 tablespoons (optional)
- Lime juice: 2 tablespoons

INSTRUCTIONS:
- Diced mangos, coconut milk, lime juice, and sweetener (if needed) should all be combined in a blender.
- Blend until creamy and smooth, stopping the blender if needed to scrape down the edges.
- If desired, add extra sweetener after tasting the mixture to adjust the sweetness.
- Leaving a small amount of space at the top for expansion, pour the mixture into the popsicle molds.
- Place the popsicle sticks into the molds, then freeze for four hours or until the popsicles are solid.
- After they have frozen, run the popsicles under some warm water for a little period to extract them from the molds.
- Serve right away or store in an airtight jar in the freezer.

DIETARY GUIDELINES FOR DIABETES:
Fresh mangoes and coconut milk are used to make these mango coconut ice pops, which naturally sweeten and provide good fats. They are suitable for those with diabetes since they employ a sugar replacement to reduce the amount of added sugar.

SHAPES AND BENEFITS:
Refreshing and exotic, mango-coconut ice pops are ideal for hot summer days. They have a creamy texture with a slight tang from the lime juice, and they're straightforward to create.

Blueberry Basil Sorbet

INGREDIENTS:
- Fresh or frozen blueberries: 2 cups
- Fresh basil leaves: 1/4 cup
- Water: 1/2 cup
- Granulated sweetener of choice: 2-3 tablespoons (optional)
- Lemon juice: 2 tablespoons

INSTRUCTIONS:
- Blend the blueberries, basil leaves, water, lemon juice, and sugar (if using) in a blender.

◇ Blend until creamy and smooth, stopping the blender if needed to scrape down the edges.
◇ If desired, add extra sweetener after tasting the mixture to adjust the sweetness.
◇ Once the mixture is in a shallow dish, freeze it for four to six hours or until it solidifies.
◇ After the sorbet has frozen, scoop it into cones or serving bowls and serve right away.

DIETARY GUIDELINES FOR DIABETES:
Fresh basil and blueberries, both high in antioxidants, combine to create a delicious and nutrient-dense sorbet. When a sugar replacement is used, the amount of added sugar is reduced, making it safe for people with diabetes.

SHAPES AND BENEFITS:
Blueberry basil sorbet blends the herbaceous flavor of basil with the sweetness of blueberries to create a distinctive and refreshing dessert option. It's simple to prepare and has a delicious harmony of savory and sweet flavors.

Pineapple Mint Granita

INGREDIENTS:
◇ Fresh pineapple, diced: 2 cups
◇ Water: 1/2 cup
◇ Granulated sweetener of choice: 2-3 tablespoons (optional)
◇ Fresh mint leaves: 1/4 cup
◇ Lime juice: 2 tablespoons

INSTRUCTIONS:
◇ Put the chopped pineapple, water, lime juice, mint leaves, and sweetener (if using) in a blender.
◇ Blend until well integrated and smooth.
◇ Transfer the blend to a low-profile dish and store it in the freezer.
◇ To get a granita texture, scrape and fluff the mixture every 30 minutes with a fork.
◇ Once the entire liquid is frozen and has a slushy consistency, keep scraping every 30 minutes.
◇ After the granita has frozen, spoon it into glasses or serving dishes and serve right away.

DIETARY GUIDELINES FOR DIABETES:
Fresh pineapple and mint are used to make this pineapple mint granita, which adds a naturally sweet and excellent taste. When a sugar replacement is used, the amount of added sugar is reduced, making it safe for people with diabetes.

FORMS AND ADVANTAGES:

Pineapple mint granita is an excellent dessert choice that's ideal for summertime cooling down. With the sweetness of pineapple and the freshness of mint, it's simple to prepare and has a pleasing texture.

Raspberry Swirl Frozen Yogurt

INGREDIENTS:
- Greek yogurt: 2 cups
- Frozen raspberries: 1 cup
- Granulated sweetener of choice: 2-3 tablespoons (optional)
- Vanilla extract: 1 teaspoon

INSTRUCTIONS:
- Blend the frozen raspberries, Greek yogurt, vanilla extract, and sweetener, if desired, in a blender.
- Blend until creamy and smooth, stopping the blender if needed to scrape down the edges.
- If desired, add extra sweetener after tasting the mixture to adjust the sweetness.
- Transfer the blend to a shallow plate and, if preferred, gently stir in extra raspberry puree.
- Freeze until solid, about 4-6 hours.
- Once frozen, transfer the yogurt to cones or serving bowls and serve right away.

DIETARY GUIDELINES FOR DIABETES:
Greek yogurt and frozen raspberries combine to create this raspberry swirl frozen yogurt, which is high in protein, probiotics, and antioxidants. When a sugar replacement is used, the amount of added sugar is reduced, making it safe for people with diabetes.

SHAPES AND BENEFITS:
The creamy texture of raspberry swirl, a tart and fruity flavor, complements frozen yogurt. The swirls of raspberry puree provide additional bursts of raspberry flavor and visual appeal.

Kiwi Lime Popsicles

INGREDIENTS:
- Kiwi, peeled and diced: 2 cups
- Lime juice: 1/4 cup
- Granulated sweetener of choice: 2-3 tablespoons (optional)
- Water: 1/2 cup

INSTRUCTIONS:
- Place the chopped kiwi, water, lime juice, and sugar (if using) in a blender.
- Blend until well integrated and smooth.
- If desired, add extra sweetener after tasting the mixture to adjust the sweetness.

◇ Leaving a small amount of space at the top for expansion, pour the mixture into the popsicle molds.
◇ Place the popsicle sticks into the molds, then freeze for four hours or until the popsicles are solid.
◇ After they have frozen, run the popsicles under some warm water for a little period to extract them from the molds.
◇ Serve right away or store in an airtight jar in the freezer.

DIETARY PLAN FOR DIABETICS:
The natural sweetness and vitamin C in these kiwi lime popsicles come from fresh kiwi and lime juice. They are suitable for those with diabetes since they employ a sugar replacement to reduce the amount of added sugar.

SHAPES AND BENEFITS:
Crisp and refreshing kiwi lime popsicles are the ideal summertime treat for hot weather. They provide a cool blast of tropical taste and are pretty simple to prepare.

Watermelon Mint Sorbet

INGREDIENTS:
◇ Seedless watermelon, diced: 4 cups
◇ Fresh mint leaves: 1/4 cup
◇ Granulated sweetener of choice: 2-3 tablespoons (optional)
◇ Lime juice: 2 tablespoons

INSTRUCTIONS:
◇ Diced watermelon, lime juice, fresh mint leaves, and sweetener (if using) should all be combined in a blender.
◇ Blend until well integrated and smooth.
◇ If desired, add extra sweetener after tasting the mixture to adjust the sweetness.
◇ Once the mixture is in a shallow dish, freeze it for four to six hours or until it solidifies.
◇ After the sorbet has frozen, scoop it into cones or serving bowls and serve right away.

DIETARY GUIDELINES FOR DIABETES:
Made with hydrating watermelon and fresh mint, this sorbet has a naturally sweet taste that is delightful. When a sugar replacement is used, the amount of added sugar is reduced, making it safe for people with diabetes.

SHAPES AND BENEFITS:
As an excellent dessert choice, watermelon mint sorbet is ideal for hot days. It is light and refreshing. It's simple to prepare and offers a refreshing mint taste along with a rush of natural sweetness.

Peach Yogurt Ice Pops

INGREDIENTS:

◇ Ripe peaches, peeled and diced: 2 cups
◇ Greek yogurt: 1 cup
◇ Granulated sweetener of choice: 2-3 tablespoons (optional)
◇ Vanilla extract: 1 teaspoon
◇ Water: 1/4 cup

INSTRUCTIONS:
◇ Greek yogurt, water, vanilla extract, sweetener (if used), and sliced peaches should all be combined in a blender.
◇ Blend until creamy and smooth, stopping the blender if needed to scrape down the edges.
◇ If desired, add extra sweetener after tasting the mixture to adjust the sweetness.
◇ Leaving a small amount of space at the top for expansion, pour the mixture into the popsicle molds.
◇ Place the popsicle sticks into the molds, then freeze for four hours or until the popsicles are solid.
◇ After they have frozen, run the popsicles under some warm water for a little period to extract them from the molds.
◇ Serve right away or store in an airtight jar in the freezer.

DIETARY GUIDELINES FOR DIABETES:
Greek yogurt and fresh peaches are used to create these peach yogurt ice pops, which naturally sweeten, protein, and probiotics. They are suitable for those with diabetes since they employ a sugar replacement to reduce the amount of added sugar.

SHAPES AND BENEFITS:
These sweet and creamy peach yogurt ice pops are the ideal treat for hot summer days. They offer a pleasing sweetness without raising blood sugar levels, and they're simple to create.

Coconut Lime Popsicles

INGREDIENTS:
◇ Coconut milk: 1 can (13.5 oz)
◇ Lime zest: 2 teaspoons
◇ Lime juice: 1/4 cup
◇ Granulated sweetener of choice: 2-3 tablespoons (optional)
◇ Shredded coconut (optional, for texture): 1/4 cup

INSTRUCTIONS:
◇ The coconut milk, lime zest, lime juice, and sweetener (if used) should all be thoroughly mixed in a bowl.
◇ Add shredded coconut if preferred for a textural boost.
◇ Leaving a small amount of space at the top for expansion, pour the mixture into the popsicle molds.
◇ Place the popsicle sticks into the molds, then freeze for four hours or until the popsicles are solid.

◇After they have frozen, run the popsicles under some warm water for a little period to extract them from the molds.
◇Serve right away or store in an airtight jar in the freezer.
DIETARY GUIDELINES FOR DIABETES:
With coconut milk and lime juice, these coconut lime popsicles offer a taste of the tropics along with healthful fats. They are suitable for those with diabetes since they employ a sugar replacement to reduce the amount of added sugar.
SHAPES AND BENEFITS:
Perfect for summertime, coconut lime popsicles provide an excellent, unique delight. They can accommodate a range of dietary requirements because they are vegan and dairy-free.

Cherry Vanilla Frozen Yogurt

INGREDIENTS:
◇Frozen cherries, pitted: 2 cups
◇Greek yogurt: 1 cup
◇Granulated sweetener of choice: 2-3 tablespoons (optional)
◇Vanilla extract: 1 teaspoon
◇Water: 1/4 cup
INSTRUCTIONS:
◇Blend the frozen cherries, Greek yogurt, water, vanilla extract, and sweetener (if desired) in a blender.
◇Blend until creamy and smooth, stopping the blender if needed to scrape down the edges.
◇If desired, add extra sweetener after tasting the mixture to adjust the sweetness.
◇Leaving a small amount of space at the top for expansion, pour the mixture into the popsicle molds.
◇Place the popsicle sticks into the molds, then freeze for four hours or until the popsicles are solid.
◇After they have frozen, run the popsicles under some warm water for a little period to extract them from the molds.
◇Serve right away or store in an airtight jar in the freezer.
DIETARY GUIDELINES FOR DIABETES:
Greek yogurt and cherries combine to create these cherry vanilla frozen yogurt popsicles, which are naturally delicious, protein-rich, and probiotic-rich. They are suitable for those with diabetes since they employ a sugar replacement to reduce the amount of added sugar.
SHAPES AND BENEFITS:
Fruity and creamy frozen yogurt popsicles with a hint of vanilla flavor are made with cherry vanilla. They offer a pleasing sweetness without raising blood sugar levels, and they're simple to create.

Pineapple Coconut Sorbet

INGREDIENTS:
- Fresh pineapple, diced: 2 cups
- Coconut milk: 1/2 cup
- Granulated sweetener of choice: 2-3 tablespoons (optional)
- Lime juice: 2 tablespoons

INSTRUCTIONS:
- Diced pineapple, coconut milk, lime juice, and sweetener (if using) should all be combined in a blender.
- Blend until well integrated and smooth.
- If desired, add extra sweetener after tasting the mixture to adjust the sweetness.
- Once the mixture is in a shallow dish, freeze it for four to six hours or until it solidifies.
- After the sorbet has frozen, scoop it into cones or serving bowls and serve right away.

DIETARY GUIDELINES FOR DIABETES:
Fresh pineapple and coconut milk are used to make this pineapple coconut sorbet, which naturally sweetens and provides good fats. When a sugar replacement is used, the amount of added sugar is reduced, making it safe for people with diabetes.

SHAPES AND BENEFITS:
On hot days, pineapple coconut sorbet is a refreshing and creamy dessert alternative that is reminiscent of a tropical paradise. It fits a range of dietary requirements because it is vegan and dairy-free.

Raspberry Mango Sorbet

INGREDIENTS:
- Frozen mango chunks: 2 cups
- Frozen raspberries: 1 cup
- Granulated sweetener of choice: 2-3 tablespoons (optional)
- Lemon juice: 2 tablespoons

INSTRUCTIONS:
- Put the frozen mango chunks, frozen raspberries, lemon juice, and sweetener (if using) in a blender.
- Blend until smooth and thoroughly blended, stopping the blender if needed to scrape down the edges.
- If desired, add extra sweetener after tasting the mixture to adjust the sweetness.
- Once the mixture is in a shallow dish, freeze it for four to six hours or until it solidifies.

◇ After the sorbet has frozen, scoop it into cones or serving bowls and serve right away.
DIETARY GUIDELINES FOR DIABETES:
Frozen mango and raspberries are used to make this raspberry mango sorbet, which adds natural sweetness and fiber. When a sugar replacement is used, the amount of added sugar is reduced, making it safe for people with diabetes.
SHAPES AND BENEFITS:
An excellent and fruity dessert choice that's ideal for hot summer days is raspberry mango sorbet. It's simple to prepare and tastes tropically sweet without making blood sugar surge.

Honeydew Mint Ice Pops

INGREDIENTS:
◇ Honeydew melon, diced: 2 cups
◇ Fresh mint leaves: 1/4 cup
◇ Granulated sweetener of choice: 2-3 tablespoons (optional)
◇ Lime juice: 2 tablespoons
INSTRUCTIONS:
◇ Put the diced honeydew melon, lime juice, fresh mint leaves, and sugar (if needed) in a blender.
◇ Blend until well integrated and smooth.
◇ If desired, add extra sweetener after tasting the mixture to adjust the sweetness.
◇ Leaving a small amount of space at the top for expansion, pour the mixture into the popsicle molds.
◇ Place the popsicle sticks into the molds, then freeze for four hours or until the popsicles are solid.
◇ After they have frozen, run the popsicles under some warm water for a little period to extract them from the molds.
◇ Serve right away or store in an airtight jar in the freezer.
DIETARY GUIDELINES FOR DIABETES:
Fresh honeydew melon and mint are used to make these honeydew mint ice pops, which naturally sweeten and have an excellent taste. They are suitable for those with diabetes since they employ a sugar replacement to reduce the amount of added sugar.
SHAPES AND BENEFITS:
Perfect for summer, honeydew mint ice pops are a refreshing and hydrating dessert alternative. They are quick and simple to prepare, and they deliver a hit of sweet and minty flavor without raising blood sugar levels.

Guilt-Free Puddings and Custards

Chia Seed Pudding

INGREDIENTS:
- Chia seeds: 1/4 cup
- Unsweetened almond milk: 1 cup
- Vanilla extract: 1/2 teaspoon
- Granulated sweetener of choice: 1-2 tablespoons (optional)

INSTRUCTIONS:
- Chia seeds, almond milk, vanilla extract, and sweetener (if used) should all be combined in a bowl.
- Mix thoroughly to blend.
- Put the bowl in the refrigerator and leave it there for at least 4 hours, or overnight, until the mixture is pudding-like in consistency.
- Before serving, stir it and add any preferred toppings, like almonds or fresh fruit.

DIETARY GUIDELINES FOR DIABETES:
Chia seed pudding is a healthy choice for those with diabetes because it's high in protein, fiber, and omega-3 fatty acids. Because of its low glycemic index, it aids with blood sugar regulation.

SHAPES AND BENEFITS:
Chia seed pudding is adaptable and may be made with different toppings and flavors. It's a simple dessert that can be made ahead of time and is both quick and healthful.

Coconut Milk Rice Pudding

INGREDIENTS:
- Arborio rice: 1/2 cup
- Coconut milk: 2 cups
- Water: 1 cup
- Granulated sweetener of choice: 2-3 tablespoons (optional)
- Vanilla extract: 1 teaspoon
- Ground cinnamon: 1/2 teaspoon

INSTRUCTIONS:
- Arborio rice, coconut milk, water, vanilla essence, ground cinnamon, and sweetener (if used) should all be combined in a pot.
- Over medium heat, bring the mixture to a simmer. Then, lower the heat to a simmer and cover the saucepan.
- Cook, stirring periodically, until the stew thickens and the rice is cooked about 25 to 30 minutes.

- Before serving, take it off the stove and allow it to cool somewhat.
- Garnish with extra cinnamon or shredded coconut, if preferred, and serve warm or cold.

DIETARY GUIDELINES FOR DIABETES:
Compared to regular rice pudding produced with dairy milk, coconut milk rice pudding is a rich, creamy dessert choice with fewer carbs. Its modest glycemic index and coconut milk give healthful fats.

SHAPES AND BENEFITS:
A classic dish is given a tropical twist with coconut milk rice pudding. It tastes good, warm or cold, and is creamy and warming. It's also acceptable for people who are lactose intolerant and free of dairy.

Pumpkin Spice Custard

INGREDIENTS:
- Canned pumpkin puree: 1 cup
- Coconut milk: 1 cup
- Eggs: 2
- Granulated sweetener of choice: 1/4 cup
- Pumpkin pie spice: 1 teaspoon
- Vanilla extract: 1 teaspoon

INSTRUCTIONS:
- Set oven temperature to 325°F, or 160°C. Four ramekins or custard cups should be lightly greased before being put on a baking dish.
- Combine the canned pumpkin puree, eggs, coconut milk, vanilla extract, sugar, and pumpkin pie spice in a bowl and mix until well combined.
- Transfer the blend to the ready-made custard cups.
- Up to halfway up the edges of the custard cups, pour hot water into the baking dish.
- Bake for 40 to 45 minutes until the custard is set through but the middle is still somewhat jiggly.
- The custard cups should be taken out of the water bath and allowed to come to room temperature.
- Place in the refrigerator to chill and solidify, preferably for two hours.
- Serve cold, with the option to top with whipped cream and pumpkin pie spice.

DIETARY GUIDELINES FOR DIABETES:
An excellent seasonal dish that is low in carbs and high in fiber is pumpkin spice custard. It has a moderate glycemic index and is made using coconut milk rather than dairy, which contributes beneficial fats.

SHAPES AND BENEFITS:
With undertones of nutmeg, cloves, and cinnamon, pumpkin spice custard has a flavor profile that is warm and comforting. It's rich, creamy, and ideal for fall or Thanksgiving dinner parties.

Chocolate Avocado Pudding

INGREDIENTS:
- Ripe avocados, peeled and pitted: 2
- Unsweetened cocoa powder: 1/2 cup
- Coconut milk: 1/2 cup
- Granulated sweetener of choice: 1/4 cup
- Vanilla extract: 1 teaspoon

INSTRUCTIONS:
- Put the peeled and pitted avocados, coconut milk, chocolate powder, sweetener, and vanilla extract in a food processor or blender.
- Blend until creamy and smooth, stopping occasionally to scrape down the sides of the processor or blender.
- After tasting the pudding, taste again and add additional sweetener if needed.
- To chill and set, move the pudding to serving dishes or jars and place them in the refrigerator for at least half an hour.
- Serve cold, with fresh berries or whipped cream as a garnish, if desired.

DIETARY GUIDELINES FOR DIABETES:
In comparison to regular chocolate pudding, chocolate avocado pudding is a delicious, creamy dessert that is lower in carbohydrates and higher in heart-healthy fats. With its modest glycemic index, it can help quell chocolate cravings without elevating blood sugar concentrations.

SHAPES AND BENEFITS:
Rich and decadent chocolate flavor and creamy texture characterize chocolate avocado pudding. It is acceptable for a range of dietary needs and is devoid of dairy and gluten.

Vanilla Bean Tapioca Pudding

INGREDIENTS:
- Tapioca pearls: 1/2 cup
- Coconut milk: 2 cups
- Water: 1 cup
- Granulated sweetener of choice: 1/4 cup
- Vanilla bean, split and seeds scraped: 1

INSTRUCTIONS:
- Tapioca pearls, coconut milk, water, sugar, and scraped vanilla bean seeds should all be combined in a pot.
- Stirring continuously; bring the mixture to a simmer over medium heat.
- After lowering the heat to low, simmer the mixture, stirring now and then, for 15 to 20 minutes, or until the tapioca pearls become transparent and the sauce thickens.
- After taking the skillet off the stove, allow the pudding to cool somewhat.

◇ If preferred, top warm or cold servings with more vanilla bean seeds.

DIETARY GUIDELINES FOR DIABETES:
Compared to regular tapioca pudding produced with dairy milk and sugar, vanilla bean tapioca pudding is a creamy and cozy dessert alternative with fewer carbs. Its modest glycemic index and coconut milk give healthful fats.

SHAPES AND BENEFITS:
With a hint of vanilla taste, vanilla bean tapioca pudding is a traditional and refined dessert choice. It's a versatile dish that goes well with any meal because it's simple to prepare and can be eaten warm or cold.

Matcha Green Tea Pudding

INGREDIENTS:
◇ Matcha green tea powder: 2 teaspoons
◇ Coconut milk: 1 can (13.5 oz)
◇ Water: 1/2 cup
◇ Granulated sweetener of choice: 2-3 tablespoons (optional)
◇ Agar agar powder: 2 teaspoons

INSTRUCTIONS:
◇ Blend matcha green tea powder, coconut milk, water, and sweetener (if desired) until a smooth consistency is achieved in a saucepan.
◇ After adding the powdered agar agar to the liquid, stir everything together.
◇ Stirring continuously; bring the mixture to a simmer over medium heat.
◇ After lowering the heat to low, simmer the mixture, stirring now and then, for around five minutes or until it thickens.
◇ Take the pudding from the stove and allow it to cool slightly.
◇ To chill and set, pour the pudding into serving plates or jars and place in the refrigerator for at least one hour.
◇ Serve cold, with fresh fruit or whipped cream as a garnish.

DIETARY GUIDELINES FOR DIABETES:
Compared to standard pudding recipes, matcha green tea pudding is a low-carbohydrate, antioxidant-rich dessert alternative. Made with matcha green tea powder and coconut milk, it offers advantageous minerals and healthy fats.

SHAPES AND BENEFITS:
Matcha green tea pudding has an earthy, somewhat sweet flavor and a vivid green hue. It is suitable for anyone with lactose intolerance or gluten sensitivity and is devoid of dairy and gluten.

Almond Joy Chia Pudding

INGREDIENTS:
◇ Chia seeds: 1/4 cup
◇ Coconut milk: 1 cup
◇ Unsweetened cocoa powder: 2 tablespoons

- ◇ Granulated sweetener of choice: 2-3 tablespoons (optional)
- ◇ Almond extract: 1/2 teaspoon
- ◇ Shredded coconut: 2 tablespoons
- ◇ Chopped almonds: 2 tablespoons

INSTRUCTIONS:
- ◇ Chia seeds, coconut milk, cocoa powder, sweetener (if used), and almond extract should all be appropriately blended in a bowl.
- ◇ Add chopped almonds and shredded coconut, and stir.
- ◇ Put the bowl in the refrigerator and leave it there for at least 4 hours, or overnight, until the mixture is pudding-like in consistency.
- ◇ Before serving, stir it and decorate it with more shredded coconut and sliced almonds.

DIETARY GUIDELINES FOR DIABETES:
Almond Joy chia pudding is a filling, high-nutrient dessert that's high in protein, fiber, and healthy fats. When consumed as part of a balanced meal plan, it can help stabilize blood sugar levels because it has a low glycemic index.

SHAPES AND BENEFITS:
Almond Joy chia pudding is a creamy, decadent dessert that combines the traditional tastes of coconut, chocolate, and almonds. It's simple to prepare and may be enhanced with different toppings for flavor and texture.

Cinnamon Maple Rice Pudding

INGREDIENTS:
- ◇ Arborio rice: 1/2 cup
- ◇ Coconut milk: 2 cups
- ◇ Water: 1 cup
- ◇ Maple syrup: 1/4 cup
- ◇ Ground cinnamon: 1 teaspoon
- ◇ Vanilla extract: 1 teaspoon

INSTRUCTIONS:
- ◇ Arborio rice, coconut milk, water, maple syrup, ground cinnamon, and vanilla essence should all be combined in a pot.
- ◇ Over medium heat, bring the mixture to a simmer. Then, lower the heat to a simmer and cover the saucepan.
- ◇ Cook, stirring periodically, until the stew thickens and the rice is cooked about 25 to 30 minutes.
- ◇ Before serving, take it off the stove and allow it to cool somewhat.
- ◇ Serve warm or cold, with the option to add a drizzle of maple syrup or a sprinkling of cinnamon as a garnish.

DIETARY GUIDELINES FOR DIABETES:

Compared to classic rice pudding recipes, cinnamon maple rice pudding has less added sugar and is a cozy and delicately sweet dessert alternative. Made with coconut milk and maple syrup, it offers natural sweetness and good fats.

SHAPES AND BENEFITS:
The flavor profile of cinnamon maple rice pudding is warm and comforting, with subtle notes of maple and cinnamon. It's rich, filling, and ideal as a dessert or as a decadent breakfast choice.

Lemon Coconut Custard Cups

INGREDIENTS:
- Eggs: 3
- Coconut milk: 1 can (13.5 oz)
- Granulated sweetener of choice: 1/4 cup
- Lemon zest: 1 tablespoon
- Lemon juice: 1/4 cup

INSTRUCTIONS:
- Set the oven's temperature to 175°C/350°F. Four ramekins or custard cups should be lightly greased before being put on a baking dish.
- Whisk the eggs, sweetener, coconut milk, zest, and juice of the lemon thoroughly in a bowl.
- Fill the prepared custard cups with the custard mixture.
- Up to halfway up the edges of the custard cups, pour hot water into the baking dish.
- Bake until the custard is set but the middle is still somewhat jiggly about 30 to 35 minutes.
- The custard cups should be taken out of the water bath and allowed to come to room temperature.
- Place in the refrigerator to chill and solidify, preferably for two hours.
- Serve cold, with the option to top with whipped cream and a lemon slice.

DIETARY GUIDELINES FOR DIABETES:
Compared to classic custard recipes, lemon coconut custard cups have fewer carbohydrates and are a zesty and refreshing dessert option. They contain vitamin C and healthy fats because they are created with fresh lemon juice and coconut milk.

SHAPES AND ADVANTAGES:
Lemon-coconut custard cups have a creamy texture and a light, acidic flavor character. They're simple to prepare and taste great as a light snack or as a fantastic dessert.

Espresso Chocolate Pots de Crème

INGREDIENTS:
- Heavy cream: 1 cup

◇ Espresso powder: 2 tablespoons
◇ Unsweetened cocoa powder: 2 tablespoons
◇ Granulated sweetener of choice: 1/4 cup
◇ Egg yolks: 3

INSTRUCTIONS:
◇ Set oven temperature to 325°F, or 160°C. In a baking dish, arrange six ramekins or custard cups.
◇ The heavy cream should be heated in a saucepan over medium heat until it starts to simmer. Take off the heat.
◇ Add the cocoa powder, sweetener, and espresso powder and whisk until completely dissolved.
◇ Smoothly whisk the egg yolks in a different basin.
◇ Pour the heated cream mixture into the egg yolks gradually while continuing to whisk to avoid curdling.
◇ To get rid of any lumps, strain the mixture into a fresh bowl using a fine-mesh sieve.
◇ Evenly distribute the mixture among the ramekins.
◇ Fill the baking dish halfway up the edges of the ramekins with boiling water.
◇ Bake for thirty to thirty-five minutes until the centers are still a little jiggly but the edges are set.
◇ Take the pots de crème out of the oven and allow them to come to room temperature.
◇ Refrigerate for a minimum of two hours or until solidified.
◇ Serve cold, with chocolate shavings and whipped cream as optional garnishes.

DIETARY GUIDELINES FOR DIABETES:
Compared to classic custard recipes, espresso chocolate pots de crème provide a rich and luscious dessert option with fewer carbohydrates. Its rich flavor and creamy texture come from the use of heavy cream, cocoa powder, and espresso powder in its recipe.

SHAPES AND BENEFITS:
With their rich chocolate and espresso flavors, espresso chocolate pots de crème provide a classy and decadent dessert experience. They are simple to prepare ahead of time for a special occasion or dinner party.

Strawberry Chia Pudding

INGREDIENTS:
◇ Chia seeds: 1/4 cup
◇ Coconut milk: 1 cup
◇ Fresh strawberries, chopped: 1/2 cup
◇ Granulated sweetener of choice: 1-2 tablespoons (optional)
◇ Vanilla extract: 1/2 teaspoon

INSTRUCTIONS:

◇ Chia seeds, coconut milk, sliced strawberries, vanilla essence, and sweetener (if used) should all be appropriately blended in a bowl.
◇ Put the bowl in the refrigerator and leave it there for at least 4 hours, or overnight, until the mixture is pudding-like in consistency.
◇ Before serving, stir it and sprinkle some more sliced strawberries on top as a garnish.

DIETARY GUIDELINES FOR DIABETES:
Rich in fiber, antioxidants, and good fats, strawberry chia pudding is a filling and healthful dessert choice. When consumed as part of a balanced meal plan, it can help stabilize blood sugar levels because it has a low glycemic index.

SHAPES AND BENEFITS:
The natural sweetness of fresh strawberries combines with the vivid and fruity flavor of strawberry chia pudding. It is acceptable for a range of dietary needs and is devoid of dairy and gluten.

Blueberry Coconut Rice Pudding

INGREDIENTS:
◇ Arborio rice: 1/2 cup
◇ Coconut milk: 2 cups
◇ Water: 1 cup
◇ Fresh blueberries: 1/2 cup
◇ Granulated sweetener of choice: 2-3 tablespoons (optional)
◇ Vanilla extract: 1 teaspoon

INSTRUCTIONS:
◇ Arborio rice, coconut milk, water, vanilla extract, fresh blueberries, and sugar (if used) should all be combined in a pot.
◇ Over medium heat, bring the mixture to a simmer. Then, lower the heat to a simmer and cover the saucepan.
◇ Cook, stirring periodically, until the stew thickens and the rice is cooked about 25 to 30 minutes.
◇ Before serving, take it off the stove and allow it to cool somewhat.
◇ Serve hot or cold, with the option to add more fresh blueberries as a garnish.

DIETARY GUIDELINES FOR DIABETES:
Compared to classic rice pudding recipes, blueberry coconut rice pudding has fewer carbohydrates and is a tasty and nutrient-rich dessert alternative. Made with fresh blueberries and coconut milk, it offers antioxidants and suitable lipids.

SHAPES AND BENEFITS:
The creamy texture and sweet flavor of blueberry coconut rice pudding are sure to please. It's a simple dish to prepare and tastes good for breakfast or dessert.

Chocolate Peanut Butter Chia Pudding

INGREDIENTS:
- Chia seeds: 1/4 cup
- Unsweetened cocoa powder: 2 tablespoons
- Peanut butter: 2 tablespoons
- Coconut milk: 1 cup
- Granulated sweetener of choice: 2-3 tablespoons (optional)

INSTRUCTIONS:
- Chia seeds, cocoa powder, peanut butter, coconut milk, and sweetener (if used) should all be appropriately blended in a bowl.
- Put the bowl in the refrigerator and leave it there for at least 4 hours, or overnight, until the mixture is pudding-like in consistency.
- Before serving, stir it and add any desired toppings, like chopped peanuts or a dollop of peanut butter.

DIETARY GUIDELINES FOR DIABETES:
Compared to standard pudding recipes, chocolate peanut butter chia pudding has fewer carbohydrates and is a filling and high-protein dessert alternative. Because peanut butter and coconut milk include healthful fats, they assist in balancing blood sugar levels.

SHAPES AND BENEFITS:
Reminiscent of a traditional dessert, chocolate peanut butter chia pudding offers a decadent and rich flavor combination. It's suitable for people with peanut allergies and is devoid of dairy and gluten.

Mango Coconut Tapioca Pudding

INGREDIENTS:
- Tapioca pearls: 1/2 cup
- Coconut milk: 2 cups
- Water: 1 cup
- Fresh mango, diced: 1 cup
- Granulated sweetener of choice: 2-3 tablespoons (optional)
- Vanilla extract: 1 teaspoon

INSTRUCTIONS:
- Tapioca pearls, coconut milk, water, mango chunks, sweetener (if using), and vanilla essence should all be combined in a pot.
- Stirring continuously; bring the mixture to a simmer over medium heat.
- After lowering the heat to low, simmer the mixture, stirring now and then, for 15 to 20 minutes, or until the tapioca pearls become transparent and the sauce thickens.
- Take the pudding from the stove and allow it to cool slightly.
- Serve warm or cold, with extra chopped mango on top if desired.

DIETARY GUIDELINES FOR DIABETES:

Compared to classic tapioca pudding recipes, mango coconut tapioca pudding has fewer carbohydrates, making it a filling and tropical dessert alternative. It has natural sweetness and healthy fats from fresh mango and coconut milk.

SHAPES AND BENEFITS:
Mango coconut tapioca pudding combines the tropical sweetness of mango with a delicious and pleasant flavor profile. It's a simple dish to prepare and goes well as a light snack or dessert.

Raspberry Almond Custard

INGREDIENTS:
- Eggs: 3
- Coconut milk: 1 can (13.5 oz)
- Granulated sweetener of choice: 1/4 cup
- Almond extract: 1/2 teaspoon
- Fresh raspberries: 1 cup

INSTRUCTIONS:
- Set the oven's temperature to 175°C/350°F. Four ramekins or custard cups should be lightly greased before being put on a baking dish.
- Beat the eggs, sweetener, coconut milk, and almond extract together in a bowl until thoroughly blended.
- Spoon half of the fresh raspberries into each custard cup.

Over the raspberries in the custard cups, pour the custard mixture.
- Up to halfway up the edges of the custard cups, pour hot water into the baking dish.
- Bake until the custard is set but the middle is still somewhat jiggly about 30 to 35 minutes.
- The custard cups should be taken out of the water bath and allowed to come to room temperature.
- Place in the refrigerator to chill and solidify, preferably for two hours.
- Serve cold, with the option to add more fresh raspberries as a garnish.

DIETARY GUIDELINES FOR DIABETES:
Compared to classic custard recipes, raspberry almond custard has fewer carbohydrates and is a fruity and creamy dessert option. Made with fresh raspberries and coconut milk, it offers antioxidants and suitable lipids.

SHAPES AND BENEFITS:
The natural sweetness of raspberries and the mild nuttiness of almond extract combine to create a delicate and elegant flavor profile for raspberry almond custard. It's a simple dish to prepare and tastes great as a dessert or special occasion treat.

Sweetened Beverages and Mocktails

Sparkling Berry Lemonade

INGREDIENTS:
- Fresh berries (such as strawberries, raspberries, or blueberries): 1 cup
- Lemon juice: 1/4 cup
- Sparkling water: 2 cups
- Granulated sweetener of choice: 2-3 tablespoons (optional)
- Ice cubes
- Fresh mint leaves for garnish

INSTRUCTIONS:
- Put the fresh berries and lemon juice in a blender. Process till smooth.
- To get rid of any seeds or pulp, strain the berry mixture through a fine-mesh screen.
- Strain the berry juice and combine it with sparkling water and sweetener (if desired) in a pitcher. Mix thoroughly until fully incorporated.
- Place ice cubes in separate glasses and cover the ice with the sparkling berry lemonade.
- Before serving, sprinkle some fresh mint leaves into each glass.

DIETARY GUIDELINES FOR DIABETES:
A hydrating and delicious beverage choice that is low in carbohydrates and free of added sugars is sparkling berry lemonade. Made with lemon juice, sparkling water, and fresh berries, it delivers vitamin C and antioxidants without raising blood sugar levels.

SHAPES AND BENEFITS:
With the fizz of sparkling water, sparkling berry lemonade has a bright, fruity flavor profile. It's ideal for serving at picnics and celebrations or simply as a cool beverage on a hot day.

Minty Iced Green Tea

INGREDIENTS:
- Green tea bags: 4
- Fresh mint leaves: 1/4 cup
- Water: 4 cups
- Granulated sweetener of choice: 2-3 tablespoons (optional)
- Ice cubes
- Lemon slices for garnish

INSTRUCTIONS:
- Heat some water in a saucepan to a boil. Take off the heat.

◇ To the heated water, add green tea bags and fresh mint leaves. Steep for five to seven minutes.
◇ Take out and dispose of the tea bags and mint leaves from the water.
◇ If using sweetener, stir until it dissolves.
◇ After letting the tea drop to room temperature, chill it in the refrigerator.
◇ Over ice cubes, pour the cold green tea.
◇ Before serving, garnish each glass with extra mint leaves and a slice of lemon.

DIETARY GUIDELINES FOR DIABETES:
A hydrating beverage option that is high in antioxidants and low in calories and carbs is minty iced green tea. Made with fresh mint leaves and green tea, it has potential blood sugar-lowering benefits as well as nutritional benefits.

SHAPES AND BENEFITS:
The delicate freshness of mint lends a refreshing flavor characteristic to this minty iced green tea. Drink it throughout the day to stay hydrated and feel more energized; it's a healthy substitute for sugary drinks.

Cucumber Lime Cooler

INGREDIENTS:
◇ Cucumber, peeled and sliced: 1
◇ Lime juice: 1/4 cup
◇ Sparkling water: 2 cups
◇ Granulated sweetener of choice: 2-3 tablespoons (optional)
◇ Ice cubes
◇ Fresh cilantro leaves for garnish

INSTRUCTIONS:
◇ Sliced cucumber and lime juice should be combined in a blender. Process till smooth.
◇ To get rid of any pulp, strain the cucumber-lime combination using a fine-mesh screen.
◇ Strain the cucumber-lime juice and combine it with sparkling water and sweetener (if desired) in a pitcher. Mix thoroughly until fully incorporated.
◇ Pour the cucumber-lime cooler over the ice cubes in each separate glass.
◇ Before serving, garnish each glass with a few fresh cilantro leaves.

DIETARY GUIDELINES FOR DIABETES:
A hydrating, low-calorie beverage alternative without additional sweets is the cucumber-lime cooler. It does not affect blood sugar levels and is created with fresh cucumber, lime juice, and sparkling water. It provides vitamins, minerals, and antioxidants.

SHAPES AND BENEFITS:

The crisp and refreshing flavor profile of cucumber lime cooler is enhanced by the tanginess of lime and the cooling effect of cucumber. Enjoy it as a healthy substitute for sugar-filled sodas and as a great way to remain hydrated in warm weather.

Watermelon Basil Lemonade

INGREDIENTS:
- Watermelon, seeded and cubed: 2 cups
- Lemon juice: 1/4 cup
- Fresh basil leaves: 1/4 cup
- Water: 2 cups
- Granulated sweetener of choice: 2-3 tablespoons (optional)
- Ice cubes
- Lemon slices and basil sprigs for garnish

INSTRUCTIONS:
- Put the watermelon cubes, lemon juice, and fresh basil leaves in a blender. Process till smooth.
- To get rid of any pulp, strain the watermelon-basil combination using a fine-mesh screen.
- Strain the watermelon-basil juice and combine it with water and honey (if desired) in a pitcher. Mix thoroughly until fully incorporated.
- Fill each glass with ice cubes, then cover the ice with the watermelon basil lemonade.
- Before serving, garnish each glass with a slice of lemon and a sprig of basil.

DIETARY GUIDELINES FOR DIABETES:
A refreshing, low-calorie beverage choice that is naturally sweetened and devoid of added sugars is watermelon basil lemonade. Made with fresh watermelon, lemon juice, and basil leaves, it offers antioxidants, vitamins, and minerals without making blood sugar surge.

SHAPES AND BENEFITS:
With the sweetness of watermelon, the sharpness of lemon, and the herbal overtones of basil, watermelon basil lemonade has a delightful and summery flavor profile. It's ideal for offering as a post-workout snack or at outdoor parties.

Peach Ginger Mocktail

INGREDIENTS:
- Fresh peaches, pitted and sliced: 2
- Fresh ginger, peeled and sliced: 1-inch piece
- Sparkling water: 2 cups
- Granulated sweetener of choice: 2-3 tablespoons (optional)
- Ice cubes

◇ Peach slices and ginger slices for garnish

INSTRUCTIONS:
◇ Put the fresh ginger and the peach slices in a blender. Process till smooth.
◇ To get rid of any fibrous parts, strain the peach-ginger combination using a fine-mesh screen.
◇ Strain the peach-ginger juice and combine it with sparkling water and sweetener (if desired) in a pitcher. Mix thoroughly until fully incorporated.
◇ Place ice cubes in each glass, then cover the ice with the peach ginger mocktail.
◇ Before serving, garnish each glass with a peach and a ginger slice.

DIETARY GUIDELINES FOR DIABETES:
A tasty and refreshing beverage choice that is low in carbs and free of added sweets is the peach ginger mocktail. It contains vitamins, minerals, and antioxidants without raising blood sugar levels because it is created with fresh peaches, ginger, and sparkling water.

SHAPES AND BENEFITS:
The natural sweetness of peaches is balanced by the warming bite of ginger in this peach ginger mocktail, which offers a harmonious blend of sweet and spicy flavors. This elegant beverage is ideal for celebratory events and serves as a cool treat on warm days.

Blueberry Lavender Lemonade

INGREDIENTS:
◇ Fresh blueberries: 1 cup
◇ Dried culinary lavender: 1 tablespoon
◇ Lemon juice: 1/4 cup
◇ Water: 2 cups
◇ Granulated sweetener of choice: 2-3 tablespoons (optional)
◇ Ice cubes
◇ Fresh blueberries and lavender sprigs for garnish

INSTRUCTIONS:
◇ Put the dried lavender, fresh blueberries, lemon juice, and water in a saucepan.
◇ Over medium heat, bring the mixture to a simmer. After that, turn the heat down to low and steep for ten to fifteen minutes.
◇ After turning off the stove, pour the blueberry-lavender mixture through a fine-mesh strainer to get rid of the particles.
◇ Strain the blueberry-lavender lemonade and, if desired, stir in the sweetener in a pitcher. Mix thoroughly until fully incorporated.
◇ Place ice cubes in separate glasses and cover the ice with the blueberry lavender lemonade.
◇ Before serving, top each glass with a sprig of lavender and some fresh blueberries.

DIETARY GUIDELINES FOR DIABETES:

Low in calories and carbs, blueberry lavender lemonade is a novel, antioxidant-rich beverage choice. Lemon juice, culinary lavender, and fresh blueberries provide vitamins, minerals, and phytonutrients without raising blood sugar levels.

SHAPES AND BENEFITS:
Blueberry lavender lemonade has a bright purple color and a subtle floral scent. The calming scent of lavender complements the delicious blueberries and tangy lemon. It's an excellent beverage that will dazzle guests at any party.

Raspberry Mint Iced Tea

INGREDIENTS:
- Fresh raspberries: 1 cup
- Fresh mint leaves: 1/4 cup
- Black tea bags: 4
- Water: 4 cups
- Granulated sweetener of choice: 2-3 tablespoons (optional)
- Ice cubes
- Fresh raspberries and mint sprigs for garnish

INSTRUCTIONS:
- Heat the water in a pot until it boils. Take off the heat.
- To the heated water, add black tea bags, fresh raspberries, and fresh mint leaves. Steep for five to seven minutes.
- To get rid of any sediments, take out the tea bags and drain the raspberry-mint tea using a fine-mesh sieve.
- Strain the raspberry-mint tea and, if desired, stir in the sweetener in a pitcher. Mix thoroughly until fully incorporated.
- After letting the tea drop to room temperature, chill it in the refrigerator.
- Over ice cubes, pour the chilled raspberry mint iced tea.
- Before serving, garnish each glass with a sprig of mint and some fresh raspberries.

DIETARY GUIDELINES FOR DIABETES:
A hydrating beverage that is high in antioxidants and low in calories and carbs is raspberry mint iced tea. This healthy drink, which contains black tea, mint leaves, and fresh raspberries, delivers vitamins, minerals, and phytonutrients without raising blood sugar levels.

SHAPES AND BENEFITS:
The acidity of raspberries counterbalances the coolness of mint in this delectable raspberry mint iced tea, which gives a delightful blend of fruity sweetness and herbal freshness. It's a multipurpose beverage that works well for both formal and informal settings.

Pineapple Coconut Refresher

INGREDIENTS:
- Fresh pineapple chunks: 1 cup
- Coconut water: 2 cups
- Lime juice: 1/4 cup
- Granulated sweetener of choice: 2-3 tablespoons (optional)
- Ice cubes
- Pineapple wedges and lime slices for garnish

INSTRUCTIONS:
- Put the lime juice, coconut water, and fresh pineapple chunks in a blender. Process till smooth.
- Blend the pineapple-coconut concoction and add sweetener (if using) to a pitcher. Mix thoroughly until fully incorporated.
- Place ice cubes in separate glasses, then cover the ice with the pineapple coconut refresher.
- Before serving, garnish each glass with a slice of lime and a pineapple.

DIETARY GUIDELINES FOR DIABETES:
A refreshing, tropical beverage that is low in calories and carbs is the pineapple coconut refresher. Made with fresh pineapple, coconut water, and lime juice, it provides electrolytes, vitamins, and minerals without making blood sugar increase.

SHAPES AND BENEFITS:
With the sweetness of pineapple, the nuttiness of coconut, and the tanginess of lime, pineapple coconut refresher offers a cool and unique flavor profile. This beverage is ideal for sipping by the pool or as a post-workout recovery drink.

Cranberry Orange Spritzer

INGREDIENTS:
- Cranberry juice, unsweetened: 1/2 cup
- Fresh orange juice: 1/2 cup
- Sparkling water: 2 cups
- Granulated sweetener of choice: 2-3 tablespoons (optional)
- Ice cubes
- Orange slices and fresh cranberries for garnish

INSTRUCTIONS:
- Combine the orange juice, cranberry juice, sparkling water, and sweetener (if using) in a pitcher. Mix thoroughly until fully incorporated.
- Place ice cubes in separate glasses, then cover the ice with the cranberry-orange spritzer.
- Before serving, top each glass with a slice of orange and a few fresh cranberries.

DIETARY GUIDELINES FOR DIABETES:
A refreshing, tart beverage that is low in calories and carbs is the cranberry orange spritzer. Made with fresh orange juice, unsweetened cranberry juice, and sparkling water, it boosts your blood sugar levels while supplying vitamins, minerals, and antioxidants.

SHAPES AND BENEFITS:
The sweetness of oranges counterbalances the sharpness of cranberries in this spritzer, which has a festive and zesty flavor profile. This is a very adaptable beverage that may be enjoyed on a daily basis or for special occasions like holidays.

Honeydew Mint Cooler

INGREDIENTS:
- Honeydew melon, peeled and cubed: 2 cups
- Fresh mint leaves: 1/4 cup
- Lime juice: 1/4 cup
- Sparkling water: 2 cups
- Granulated sweetener of choice: 2-3 tablespoons (optional)
- Ice cubes
- Honeydew melon balls and fresh mint sprigs for garnish

INSTRUCTIONS:
- Put the lime juice, fresh mint leaves, and honeydew melon cubes in a blender. Process till smooth.
- Blend the honeydew-mint concoction and add the sparkling water and sweetener (if using) to a pitcher. Mix thoroughly until fully incorporated.
- Place ice cubes in separate glasses, then cover the ice with the honeydew mint cooler.
- Before serving, garnish each glass with a sprig of mint and balls of honeydew melon.

DIETARY GUIDELINES FOR DIABETES:
A hydrating, calorie- and carbohydrate-free beverage alternative is the honeydew mint cooler. Made with fresh honeydew melon, lime juice, mint leaves, and sparkling water, it offers antioxidants, vitamins, and minerals without raising blood sugar levels.

SHAPES AND BENEFITS:
The sweetness of honeydew melon and the reviving scent of mint combine to create a flavor profile that is both cooling and revitalizing. It's a lovely drink that's great as a fruity and light substitute for sugary sodas or to enjoy on a hot summer day.

Strawberry Basil Lemonade

INGREDIENTS:
- Fresh strawberries, hulled and sliced: 1 cup

◇ Fresh basil leaves: 1/4 cup
◇ Lemon juice: 1/4 cup
◇ Water: 2 cups
◇ Granulated sweetener of choice: 2-3 tablespoons (optional)
◇ Ice cubes
◇ Strawberry slices and basil leaves for garnish

INSTRUCTIONS:
◇ Sliced strawberries, lemon juice, and fresh basil leaves should all be combined in a blender. Process till smooth.
◇ Blend the strawberry-basil mixture and add water and sweetener (if using) to a pitcher. Mix thoroughly until fully incorporated.
◇ Place ice cubes in separate glasses and cover the ice with the strawberry basil lemonade.
◇ Before serving, garnish each glass with a strawberry slice and a basil leaf.

DIETARY GUIDELINES FOR DIABETES:
A tasty, high-antioxidant, low-calorie, and carbohydrate beverage option is strawberry basil lemonade. Made with water, lemon juice, fresh strawberries, and basil leaves, it provides vitamins, minerals, and phytonutrients without raising blood sugar levels.

SHAPES AND BENEFITS:
The natural sweetness of strawberries is balanced by the fragrant freshness of basil in this exquisite blend of sweet and herbal aromas that is strawberry basil lemonade. This elegant beverage is ideal for hosting guests or sipping on for a revitalizing pick-me-up.

Mango Pineapple Punch

INGREDIENTS:
◇ Fresh mango chunks: 1 cup
◇ Fresh pineapple chunks: 1 cup
◇ Orange juice: 1/2 cup
◇ Pineapple juice: 1/2 cup
◇ Sparkling water: 2 cups
◇ Granulated sweetener of choice: 2-3 tablespoons (optional)
◇ Ice cubes
◇ Mango slices and pineapple chunks for garnish

INSTRUCTIONS:
◇ Put the pineapple chunks, orange juice, and pineapple chunks in a blender. Process till smooth.
◇ Blend the mango-pineapple concoction and add the sparkling water and sweetener (if using) to a pitcher. Mix thoroughly until fully incorporated.
◇ Place ice cubes in separate glasses and cover the ice with the mango-pine punch.

◇ Before serving, garnish each glass with a piece of pineapple and a slice of mango.

DIETARY GUIDELINES FOR DIABETES:
A refreshing, tropical beverage that is low in calories and carbs is mango pineapple punch. It is produced with fresh pineapple, orange juice, pineapple juice, sparkling water, and mango. It provides antioxidants, vitamins, and minerals without raising blood sugar levels.

SHAPES AND BENEFITS:
Mango pineapple punch combines the tanginess of pineapple with the sweetness of mango to create a tropical flavor explosion. This festive beverage is ideal as a refreshing treat on a hot day or for luau-themed gatherings.

Kiwi Coconut Cooler

INGREDIENTS:
◇ Kiwi, peeled and sliced: 2
◇ Coconut water: 2 cups
◇ Lime juice: 1/4 cup
◇ Sparkling water: 2 cups
◇ Granulated sweetener of choice: 2-3 tablespoons (optional)
◇ Ice cubes
◇ Kiwi slices and lime wedges for garnish

INSTRUCTIONS:
◇ Put the lime juice, coconut water, and sliced kiwi in a blender. Process till smooth.
◇ Blend the kiwi-coconut concoction and add the sparkling water and sweetener (if using) to a pitcher. Mix thoroughly until fully incorporated.
◇ Place ice cubes into separate glasses and cover the ice with the kiwi coconut cooler.
◇ Before serving, garnish each glass with a lime wedge and a piece of kiwi.

DIETARY GUIDELINES FOR DIABETES:
Kiwi Coconut Cooler is a low-calorie, high-electrolyte beverage that is pleasant and low in carbs. Made with fresh kiwi, lime juice, coconut water, and sparkling water, it's low in sugar and high in vitamins, minerals, and hydration.

SHAPES AND BENEFITS:
The acidity of kiwis and the mild sweetness of coconut water combine to create a tropical and energizing taste profile for the Kiwi Coconut Cooler. This refreshing beverage is ideal for restoring electrolytes after physical activity or as a fruity, light substitute for sugary drinks.

Blackberry Mint Mocktail

INGREDIENTS:

- Fresh blackberries: 1 cup
- Fresh mint leaves: 1/4 cup
- Lemon juice: 1/4 cup
- Sparkling water: 2 cups
- Granulated sweetener of choice: 2-3 tablespoons (optional)
- Ice cubes
- Blackberries and mint sprigs for garnish

INSTRUCTIONS:
- Blend the blackberries, mint leaves, and lemon juice in a blender.
- Process till smooth.
- Blend the blackberry-mint concoction and add sparkling water and sweetener (if using) to a pitcher. Mix thoroughly until fully incorporated.
- Place ice cubes in separate glasses, then cover the ice with the blackberry mint mocktail.
- Before serving, garnish each glass with a blackberry and a sprig of mint.

DIETARY GUIDELINES FOR DIABETES:
A delightful and antioxidant-rich beverage choice that is minimal in calories and carbs is the blackberry mint mocktail. Made with fresh blackberries, mint leaves, lemon juice, and sparkling water, it replenishes your blood sugar without raising your levels of vitamins, minerals, or phytonutrients.

SHAPES AND BENEFITS:
The sweetness of blackberries and the reviving scent of mint combine to create a blackberry mint mocktail that bursts with delicious and aromatic sensations. This refined beverage is ideal as a light and refreshing treat or for special events.

Grapefruit Rosemary Spritzer

INGREDIENTS:
- Fresh grapefruit juice: 1/2 cup
- Fresh rosemary sprigs: 2
- Sparkling water: 2 cups
- Granulated sweetener of choice: 2-3 tablespoons (optional)
- Ice cubes
- Grapefruit slices and rosemary sprigs for garnish

INSTRUCTIONS:
- Sparkling water, grapefruit juice, fresh rosemary sprigs, and sweetener (if used) should all be combined in a pitcher. Mix thoroughly until fully incorporated.
- Fill each glass with ice cubes, then cover the ice with the grapefruit rosemary spritzer.
- Before serving, garnish each glass with a grapefruit slice and a rosemary sprig.

DIETARY GUIDELINES FOR DIABETES:

A calorie- and carbohydrate-efficient, vitamin-rich beverage choice is the grapefruit rosemary spritzer. Made with fresh grapefruit juice, sprigs of rosemary, and sparkling water, it provides antioxidants, vitamins, and minerals without raising blood sugar.

SHAPES AND BENEFITS:
The acidity of grapefruit and the heady perfume of rosemary combine to create a sophisticated and herbaceous flavor profile in the grapefruit rosemary spritzer. This light and zesty beverage is ideal for brunches or as a refreshing substitute for heavy drinks.

Special Occasion Desserts:

Flourless Chocolate Torte

INGREDIENTS:
- 8 ounces dark chocolate, chopped
- 1/2 cup unsalted butter
- 3/4 cup granulated sugar or preferred sweetener
- three large eggs
- one teaspoon vanilla extract
- Pinch of salt

STEP-BY-STEP INSTRUCTIONS:
- Set oven temperature to 175°C/350°F. Line the bottom of a 9-inch round cake pan with parchment paper and grease it.
- Melt the butter and chocolate together in a heatproof bowl over a pot of simmering water, stirring to ensure smoothness.
- Take off the heat and stir in the sugar until it dissolves.
- One egg at a time, whisk in until thoroughly blended.
- Mix in the salt and vanilla extract.
- After filling the pan, level the top with the batter.
- Bake for 25 to 30 minutes or until moist crumbs come out of a toothpick inserted in the center.
- After 10 minutes of cooling in the pan, move the contents to a wire rack to finish cooling.

DIABETES DIETARY GUIDELINES:
This flourless chocolate torte is excellent for those with diabetes because it is gluten-free and low in carbs. As part of a balanced diet, it can be consumed in moderation and offers reasonable levels of protein and fat.

SHAPES AND BENEFITS:
Packed with a rich, decadent chocolate taste and a dense, fudgy texture, this dish is perfect for people with diabetes who watch portion sizes.

Tiramisu Parfaits

INGREDIENTS:
- 1 cup brewed coffee, cooled
- two tablespoons coffee liqueur (optional)
- 1/2 cup mascarpone cheese
- 1/2 cup plain Greek yogurt
- two tablespoons honey or preferred sweetener
- 1/2 teaspoon vanilla extract
- Ladyfingers or sponge cake, cut into cubes
- Cocoa powder for dusting

STEP-BY-STEP INSTRUCTIONS:
- Pour the brewed coffee and, if desired, coffee liqueur into a shallow dish.
- Mascarpone cheese, Greek yogurt, honey, and vanilla essence should all be combined in a bowl and whisked until smooth.
- Arrange the mascarpone mixture and soak ladyfingers or sponge cake cubes in alternate layers in serving glasses or jars.
- Once the glasses are full, continue layering until the mascarpone mixture reaches the top.
- Sprinkle chocolate powder on top.
- Before serving, cover and chill for at least two hours or overnight.

DIABETES DIETARY GUIDELINES:
Using Greek yogurt and mascarpone cheese instead of ladyfingers and sugar reduces the amount of carbohydrates in this tiramisu parfait dish. When included in a balanced diet and consumed in moderation, it offers calcium and protein.

FORMS AND ADVANTAGES:
It is a decadent, creamy dessert with layers of tastes enhanced by coffee that is reduced in carbs compared to conventional tiramisu and is perfect for people with diabetes.

Raspberry Swirl Cheesecake

INGREDIENTS:
- 1 1/2 cups almond flour
- 1/4 cup unsalted butter, melted
- 16 ounces cream cheese, softened
- 1/2 cup granulated sugar or preferred sweetener
- two large eggs
- one teaspoon vanilla extract
- 1/2 cup raspberry puree (fresh or thawed frozen raspberries)

STEP-BY-STEP INSTRUCTIONS:
- Turn the oven on to 325°F, or 160°C. In a 9-inch springform pan, grease it.
- Melted butter and almond flour should be thoroughly mixed in a bowl.
- Fill the prepared pan bottom with the mixture by pressing.
- Cream cheese and sugar should be thoroughly mixed in a different basin.
- Add one egg at a time, beating thoroughly after each addition.
- Add vanilla extract and stir.
- Cover the crust with the cream cheese mixture.
- Drizzle with raspberry puree and use a knife to swirl it around.
- Bake for 45 to 50 minutes, or until the center is still somewhat jiggly, but the outside is set.
- Allow to cool in the pan on a wire rack, then chill in the refrigerator until ready to serve, at least 4 hours.

DIABETES DIETARY GUIDELINES:
Using an almond flour crust and sugar-free sweetener, this raspberry swirl cheesecake has fewer carbohydrates than a typical cheesecake. As part of a balanced diet, it can be consumed in moderation and offers protein.
SHAPES AND BENEFITS:
Low in carbohydrates compared to classic cheesecake, this creamy cheesecake with a tart raspberry swirl is ideal for people with diabetes.

Chocolate-Dipped Strawberries

INGREDIENTS:
- Fresh strawberries, rinsed and dried
- 4 ounces dark chocolate, chopped
- one teaspoon coconut oil

STEP-BY-STEP INSTRUCTIONS:
- Use parchment paper to line a baking sheet.
- Melt the chocolate and coconut oil in a heatproof bowl over a saucepan of simmering water, stirring to ensure smoothness.
- Each strawberry should be dipped halfway into the molten chocolate.
- Arrange the dipped strawberries onto the ready baking sheet.
- Chill for fifteen to twenty minutes or until the chocolate hardens.

DIABETES DIETARY GUIDELINES:
As a dessert alternative, these chocolate-dipped strawberries have fewer carbohydrates than store-bought candies and chocolates. They can be included in a balanced diet and, when consumed in moderation, offer the antioxidants found in dark chocolate.

SHAPES AND BENEFITS:
Rich dark chocolate-covered fresh and juicy strawberries are fewer in carbs than standard chocolate sweets, making them a good choice for people with diabetes.

Red Velvet Cake Bites

INGREDIENTS:
- 1 1/2 cups almond flour
- 1/4 cup unsweetened cocoa powder
- one teaspoon baking powder
- 1/4 teaspoon salt
- 1/2 cup unsalted butter, softened
- 1/2 cup granulated sugar or preferred sweetener
- two large eggs
- one teaspoon vanilla extract
- 1/2 cup unsweetened almond milk
- one tablespoon of red food coloring

◇ Cream cheese frosting (store-bought or homemade) for dipping (optional)

STEP-BY-STEP INSTRUCTIONS:

◇ Set oven temperature to 175°C/350°F. Line a 9x9-inch baking pan with parchment paper, allowing overhang on the sides, and grease the pan.
◇ Mix the almond flour, baking powder, cocoa powder, and salt in a bowl.
◇ Beat sugar and butter together in another basin until frothy and light.
◇ Add one egg at a time, beating thoroughly after each addition.
◇ Add vanilla extract and stir.
◇ Add the dry ingredients to the butter mixture gradually, starting and finishing with the dry components and alternating with almond milk.
◇ Add red food coloring and stir until fully incorporated.
◇ Fill the baking pan with batter, spreading evenly.
◇ When a toothpick put into the center comes out clean, bake for 20 to 25 minutes.
◇ Allow the pan to cool fully on a wire rack.
◇ Cut out cake bits from the cooled cake using a small cookie cutter.
◇ Not required: Cake pieces can be dipped in cream cheese icing.

DIABETES DIETARY GUIDELINES:

Compared to regular red velvet cake, the carbohydrate level of these bite-sized pieces of red velvet cake is lower because they are created with almond flour and sugar-free sweetener. As part of a balanced diet, they can be eaten in moderation and offer protein.

FORMS AND ADVANTAGES:

Small red velvet cake bites are better for people with diabetes because they have fewer carbs than regular cake.

Hazelnut Mousse with Dark Chocolate Drizzle

INGREDIENTS:

◇ 1/2 cup hazelnuts
◇ 1 cup heavy cream
◇ two tablespoons honey or preferred sweetener
◇ 4 ounces dark chocolate, chopped
◇ one teaspoon coconut oil

STEP-BY-STEP INSTRUCTIONS:

◇ Set oven temperature to 175°C/350°F. Arrange the hazelnuts on a baking sheet in a single layer.
◇ For 8 to 10 minutes, or until aromatic and gently browned, toast the hazelnuts in the oven.
◇ Once the hazelnuts have cooled down a bit, remove the skins by rubbing them with a fresh kitchen towel.
◇ Pulverize the hazelnuts into a fine powder using a blender or food processor.

◇ Beat heavy cream and honey together in a bowl until firm peaks form.
◇ Till thoroughly blended, gently mix in the ground hazelnuts into the whipped cream.
◇ Pour hazelnut mousse into bowls or serving glasses.
◇ Melt the chocolate and coconut oil in a heatproof bowl over a saucepan of simmering water, stirring to ensure smoothness.
◇ Pour chocolate that has melted over the hazelnut mousse.
◇ Before serving, place in the refrigerator for at least one hour.

DIETARY GUIDELINES FOR DIABETES:
Made with heavy cream and honey, this hazelnut mousse has a moderate protein and carbohydrate content. When consumed in moderation as part of a balanced diet, it has fewer carbs than typical desserts.

SHAPES AND BENEFITS:
Protein and vital nutrients are provided by this light and airy hazelnut mousse with a decadent chocolate drizzle, making it a good choice for people with diabetes.

Lemon Blueberry Trifle

INGREDIENTS:
◇ 1 1/2 cups blueberries
◇ one tablespoon lemon juice
◇ two tablespoons honey or preferred sweetener
◇ 1 1/2 cups plain Greek yogurt
◇ 1/2 teaspoon vanilla extract
◇ 1 cup almond biscotti or pound cake, cubed
◇ Lemon zest, for garnish (optional)

STEP-BY-STEP INSTRUCTIONS:
◇ Toss blueberries, honey, and lemon juice in a bowl until well coated.
◇ Smoothly blend Greek yogurt and vanilla extract in a different bowl.
◇ Arrange the pound cake cubes or almond biscotti in serving glasses or jars, then top with a layer of Greek yogurt mixture and a layer of blueberry mixture.
◇ Continue layering until the glasses are complete; finally, top with a layer of Greek yogurt mixture.
◇ If desired, garnish with lemon zest.
◇ Before serving, cover and chill for at least one hour.

DIABETES DIETARY GUIDELINES:
Greek yogurt and honey are used to make this lemon blueberry trifle, which offers moderate levels of carbohydrates and protein. When consumed in moderation as part of a balanced diet, it has less sugar than typical trifles.

SHAPES AND BENEFITS:
Rich Greek yogurt with layers of flavorful lemon and blueberries, this dish offers vital nutrients and protein, making it an excellent choice for people with diabetes.

Pistachio Rosewater Semifreddo

INGREDIENTS:
- 1/2 cup shelled pistachios
- 1 cup heavy cream
- two tablespoons honey or preferred sweetener
- one teaspoon of rosewater
- Pistachios, chopped, for garnish (optional)

STEP-BY-STEP INSTRUCTIONS:
- Pistachios should be ground into a fine powder in a blender or food processor.
- Beat heavy cream and honey together in a bowl until firm peaks form.
- Till thoroughly blended, gently fold in the ground pistachios and rosewater into the whipped cream.
- Transfer the pistachio rosewater mixture into a plastic wrap-lined loaf pan.
- Refine the surface using a spatula.
- Place a plastic wrap over it and freeze for a minimum of 4 hours or until solid.
- Turn the semifreddo over onto a serving tray and take off the plastic wrapper before serving.
- If desired, add chopped pistachios as a garnish.

DIABETES DIETARY GUIDELINES:
Made with heavy cream and honey, this pistachio rosewater semifreddo has a modest carbohydrate content. When consumed in moderation as part of a balanced diet, it has less sugar than typical desserts.

SHAPES AND BENEFITS:
Protein and vital nutrients are provided by this light, creamy semifreddo, which tastes delicately of pistachios and rosewater and is ideal for people with diabetes.

Coconut Cream Pie with Almond Crust

INGREDIENTS:
- 1 1/2 cups almond flour
- 1/4 cup unsweetened shredded coconut
- 1/4 cup unsalted butter, melted
- 1/4 cup honey or preferred sweetener
- 2 cups coconut milk
- 1/4 cup cornstarch
- 1/4 cup honey or preferred sweetener
- one teaspoon vanilla extract
- Toasted coconut flakes for garnish (optional)

STEP-BY-STEP INSTRUCTIONS:

◇ Set oven temperature to 175°C/350°F. Pat a 9-inch pie dish clean.
◇ Almond flour, shredded coconut, melted butter, and honey should all be thoroughly mixed in a bowl.
◇ Fill the prepared pie plate with the mixture, pressing it up the sides and into the bottom.
◇ Bake for 12 to 15 minutes until the color turns golden.
◇ Allow to cool fully on a wire rack.
◇ Combine the coconut milk, cornstarch, honey, and vanilla extract in a saucepan and stir until well combined.
◇ Stirring continually, cook over medium heat until the mixture thickens.
◇ Fill the chilled almond crust with filling.
◇ Chill for a minimum of two hours or until solidified.
◇ If preferred, top with toasted coconut flakes right before serving.

DIABETES DIETARY GUIDELINES:
Using an almond flour crust and sugar-free sweetener, this coconut cream pie has fewer carbohydrates than other pies. It can be included in a balanced diet and enjoyed in moderation since it delivers healthy fats from coconut milk.

SHAPES AND BENEFITS:
With fewer carbs than regular pies, this creamy coconut filling with a nutty almond shell is ideal for people with diabetes.

Salted Caramel Chocolate Pots de Crème

INGREDIENTS:
◇ 6 ounces dark chocolate, chopped
◇ 1 cup heavy cream
◇ 1/4 cup honey or preferred sweetener
◇ four large egg yolks
◇ 1/2 teaspoon vanilla extract
◇ Flaky sea salt for garnish

STEP-BY-STEP INSTRUCTIONS:
◇ Turn the oven on to 325°F, or 160°C. In a baking dish, arrange six ramekins.
◇ Melt chocolate, heavy cream, and honey in a heatproof dish over a pot of simmering water, stirring to ensure smoothness.
◇ Beat the egg yolks and vanilla extract together thoroughly in another basin.
◇ Whisk continuously as you slowly add the chocolate mixture into the egg yolks.
◇ Pour mixture into a fresh bowl after straining through a fine-mesh strainer.
◇ Split the mixture amongst the ramekins.
◇ Halfway up the ramekin sides and pour hot water into the baking dish.

◇ Bake for 25 to 30 minutes, or until the centers are still a little jiggly, but the edges are set.
◇ Take out of the oven and allow to cool for ten minutes in the water bath.
◇ Place the ramekins on a wire rack to finish cooling.
◇ Chill in the refrigerator for a minimum of two hours.
◇ Add a dash of flaky sea salt to each pot de crème before serving.

DIABETES DIETARY GUIDELINES:
Made with heavy cream and honey, these salted caramel chocolate pots de crème have a modest carbohydrate content. When included in moderation as part of a balanced diet, they can be enjoyed in moderation and have less sugar than typical desserts.

SHAPES AND BENEFITS:
Low in carbohydrates compared to usual sweets, this silky and rich chocolate custard is perfect for those with diabetes. It also has a taste of salted caramel.

Bonus Recipes

Sugar-Free Vanilla Frosting

INGREDIENTS:
- 1 cup unsalted butter, softened
- 3 cups powdered erythritol or preferred sugar-free sweetener
- two teaspoons vanilla extract
- 2-4 tablespoons heavy cream or almond milk

STEP-BY-STEP INSTRUCTIONS:
- Softened butter should be beaten until creamy in a mixing bowl.
- Add the powdered erythritol gradually while beating until smooth and well-mixed.
- Add vanilla extract and stir.
- One tablespoon at a time, add heavy cream or almond milk until the required consistency is achieved.
- Frosting should be light and fluffy after two to three minutes of medium-high pace beating.
- Store in the fridge for later use, or use right away to frost cakes or cupcakes.

DIABETES DIETARY GUIDELINES:
I used erythritol, a sugar alcohol that doesn't spike blood sugar, to make this sugar-free vanilla frosting. When included in a balanced diet and consumed in moderation, it can be beneficial for those with diabetes.

SHAPES AND BENEFITS:
Sugar-free, classic vanilla taste frosting that is light and fluffy and ideal for those with diabetes.

Cream Cheese Frosting with Stevia

INGREDIENTS:
- 8 ounces cream cheese, softened
- 1/2 cup unsalted butter, softened
- 2-3 cups powdered stevia or preferred sugar-free sweetener
- one teaspoon vanilla extract

STEP-BY-STEP INSTRUCTIONS:
- Beat butter and softened cream cheese until smooth and creamy in a mixing basin.
- Add the stevia powder gradually, beating until smooth and thoroughly blended.
- Add vanilla extract and stir.
- Frosting should be light and fluffy after two to three minutes of medium-high pace beating.

◇ Store in the fridge for later use, or use right away to frost cakes or cupcakes.

DIABETES DIETARY GUIDELINES:
This stevia-infused cream cheese frosting is sugar-free and great for those with diabetes. When included in moderation as part of a balanced diet, it offers a lower-carb substitute for traditional frosting.

FORMS AND ADVANTAGES:
Sugar-free, rich, creamy frosting with a tangy cream cheese flavor is ideal for those with diabetes.

Homemade Whipped Cream with Coconut Milk

INGREDIENTS:
◇ one can (13.5 ounces) full-fat coconut milk, chilled overnight
◇ 1-2 tablespoons powdered erythritol or preferred sugar-free sweetener
◇ one teaspoon vanilla extract

STEP-BY-STEP INSTRUCTIONS:
◇ Beaters and a mixing bowl should be chilled in the fridge for at least fifteen minutes.
◇ Crack open the chilled coconut milk can and remove the solid coconut cream, leaving the liquid behind, into the cold mixing bowl.
◇ Use a high-speed mixer to beat the coconut cream until soft peaks form.
◇ Vanilla extract and powdered erythritol should be added gradually while beating until firm peaks form.
◇ Store in the fridge for later use, or use right away as a topping for sweets.

DIABETES DIETARY GUIDELINES:
When incorporated into a balanced diet and consumed in moderation, this sugar-free, homemade whipped cream with coconut milk is appropriate for those with diabetes. It offers a dairy-free substitute for regular whipped cream.

SHAPES AND BENEFITS:
Dairy-free, sugar-free, light whipped cream with a hint of coconut flavor that's perfect for people with diabetes.

Dark Chocolate Ganache

INGREDIENTS:
◇ 8 ounces dark chocolate, chopped
◇ 1 cup heavy cream
◇ 1-2 tablespoons powdered erythritol or preferred sugar-free sweetener (optional)

STEP-BY-STEP INSTRUCTIONS:
◇ Put chopped dark chocolate in a basin that can withstand heat.

◇ Heat the heavy cream in a saucepan over medium heat until it begins to steam, but do not boil.
◇ After adding the hot cream to the chopped chocolate, wait two to three minutes.
◇ Mix the blend until it becomes glossy and smooth. Add sweetener or powdered erythritol to taste if desired.
◇ Ganache should cool slightly before glazing cakes or other pastries.
◇ Use right away or put in the fridge to use at a later time. Before using, if refrigerated, gently reheat.

DIABETES DIETARY GUIDELINES:
You can use erythritol or another sugar-free sweetener to make this dark chocolate ganache sugar-free. When incorporated into a healthy diet and consumed in moderation, it offers a decadent and rich topping for desserts.

FORMS AND ADVANTAGES:
Silky and glossy chocolate ganache is ideal for people with diabetes since it contains no added sugar when made with erythritol.

Fresh Fruit Compote

INGREDIENTS:
2 cups fresh mixed berries (such as strawberries, blueberries, raspberries)
Two tablespoons water
1-2 tablespoons powdered erythritol or preferred sugar-free sweetener
One teaspoon of lemon juice

STEP-BY-STEP INSTRUCTIONS:
◇ Add the fresh berries, water, erythritol powder, and lemon juice to a saucepan.
◇ Simmer on medium heat, stirring periodically, for 5 to 7 minutes, or until the berries start to release their juices and the sauce starts to get a little thicker.
◇ Before serving, remove from the heat and allow the compote to cool somewhat.
◇ Serve hot or cold on top of yogurt, pastries, or pancakes for dessert.

DIABETES DIETARY GUIDELINES:
When consumed in moderation as part of a balanced diet, this fresh fruit compote is ideal for those with diabetes because it is naturally sweetened with erythritol or a sugar-free sweetener. Fresh berries include fiber, vitamins, and minerals.

FORMS AND ADVANTAGES:
It is bursting with aromas of fresh fruit, low in carbs, naturally sweetened, and ideal for people with diabetes.

Sugar-Free Caramel Sauce

INGREDIENTS:

- 1 cup heavy cream
- 1/2 cup powdered erythritol or preferred sugar-free sweetener
- two tablespoons unsalted butter
- one teaspoon vanilla extract
- Pinch of salt

STEP-BY-STEP INSTRUCTIONS:

- Stir the powdered erythritol and heavy cream in a saucepan over medium heat until the erythritol dissolves.
- After bringing the mixture to a simmer, lower the heat to a simmer and let it cook for 30 to 40 minutes, stirring now and then until it thickens.
- Take off the heat and mix in the butter, vanilla essence, and a small amount of salt.
- Before serving, allow the caramel sauce to cool somewhat.
- Any caramel sauce leftovers should be refrigerated and then gently warmed up before using.

DIABETES DIETARY GUIDELINES:
Erythritol is used to make this sugar-free caramel sauce, which offers a reduced-carb substitute for regular caramel sauce. When included in a balanced diet and consumed in moderation, it can be beneficial for those with diabetes.

SHAPES AND BENEFITS:
Sugar-free, rich, decadent caramel flavor that's good for people with diabetes.

Lemon Glaze with Monk Fruit Sweetener

INGREDIENTS:

- 1 cup powdered monk fruit sweetener or preferred sugar-free sweetener
- 2-3 tablespoons fresh lemon juice
- one teaspoon lemon zest

STEP-BY-STEP INSTRUCTIONS:

- Combine fresh lemon juice, zest, and powdered monk fruit sweetener in a bowl and stir until smooth.
- If necessary, adjust the consistency by adding extra lemon juice.
- Drizzle over cakes, cupcakes, or cookies right away.
- Any leftover glaze can be kept in the fridge for up to a week in an airtight container.

DIABETES DIETARY GUIDELINES:
Using monk fruit sweetener, this lemon glaze offers a sugar-free substitute for conventional glazes. When included in a balanced diet and consumed in moderation, it can be beneficial for those with diabetes.

SHAPES AND BENEFITS:
Sugar-free, tangy lemon flavor that is enjoyable for people with diabetes.

Chocolate Avocado Mousse

INGREDIENTS:
- two ripe avocados
- 1/4 cup unsweetened cocoa powder
- 1/4 cup powdered erythritol or preferred sugar-free sweetener
- 2-4 tablespoons unsweetened almond milk
- one teaspoon vanilla extract
- Pinch of salt

STEP-BY-STEP INSTRUCTIONS:
- Scoop the avocado flesh into a food processor or blender.
- Add the almond milk, vanilla extract, cocoa powder, and erythritol powder, along with a dash of salt.
- Scrape down the sides as necessary, and blend until creamy and smooth.
- If necessary, adjust the consistency by adding extra almond milk.
- Spoon mousse into dishes or glasses for serving.
- Before serving, let the food cool for at least half an hour in the refrigerator.

DIABETES DIETARY GUIDELINES:
Erythritol is used to sweeten this chocolate avocado mousse naturally, and it also contains healthy fats from avocados. When included in a balanced diet and consumed in moderation, it can be beneficial for those with diabetes.

SHAPES AND BENEFITS:
Naturally sweetened, this rich, creamy chocolate mousse has a hint of avocado flavor and is safe for people with diabetes.

Almond Buttercream Frosting

INGREDIENTS:
- 1 cup unsalted butter, softened
- 3 cups powdered erythritol or preferred sugar-free sweetener
- one teaspoon of almond extract
- 2-4 tablespoons heavy cream or almond milk

STEP-BY-STEP INSTRUCTIONS:
- Softened butter should be beaten until creamy in a mixing bowl.
- Add the powdered erythritol gradually while beating until smooth and well-mixed.
- Add almond extract and stir.
- One tablespoon at a time, add heavy cream or almond milk until the required consistency is achieved.
- Frosting should be light and fluffy after two to three minutes of medium-high pace beating.
- Store in the fridge for later use, or use right away to frost cakes or cupcakes.

DIABETES DIETARY GUIDELINES:

Sugar-free and safe for those with diabetes, this almond buttercream frosting should only be used in moderation as part of a balanced diet. It gives cakes and cupcakes a lovely almond flavor and works well as a frosting.

SHAPES AND BENEFITS:
Sugar-free, creamy, smooth frosting with a bit of almond taste that's perfect for people with diabetes.

Vanilla Bean Pastry Cream

INGREDIENTS:
- 2 cups whole milk
- one vanilla bean, split lengthwise and seeds scraped out
- four large egg yolks
- 1/2 cup powdered erythritol or preferred sugar-free sweetener
- 1/4 cup cornstarch
- Pinch of salt

STEP-BY-STEP INSTRUCTIONS:
- Heat whole milk and the pod and seeds of the vanilla bean in a saucepan over medium heat until steaming but not boiling.
- Egg yolks, cornstarch, powdered erythritol, and a small amount of salt should all be combined in a mixing basin and whisked until smooth and light.
- Whisk continuously as you gradually add the heated milk liquid into the egg yolk mixture.
- Put the mixture back in the pot and simmer it over medium heat for five to seven minutes, whisking continually until it thickens.
- Take off the heat source and dispose of the vanilla bean pod.
- To avoid skin from forming, transfer the pastry cream to a bowl and cover it with plastic wrap, pressing it immediately onto the top.
- Before using, let it cool in the refrigerator for at least two hours.

DIABETES DIETARY GUIDELINES:
Used sparingly as part of a balanced diet, this sugar-free vanilla bean pastry cream is appropriate for those with diabetes. It gives cakes, pastries, and desserts a thick, creamy filling.

SHAPES AND BENEFITS:
A sugar-free, vanilla bean-flavored pastry cream that is smooth and velvety and ideal for people with diabetes.

Conclusion and Final Tips for Diabetic Dessert Success

Now that we have reached the end of our exploration of diabetic sweets, it is time to take stock of the knowledge gained, the tastes enjoyed, and the victories attained. In this last chapter, we provide some closing thoughts, comments, and priceless advice to ensure that you continue to make and enjoy sweets that are suitable for people with diabetes.

CELEBRATING PROGRESS, NOT PERFECTION

EMBRACING IMPERFECTION:
Assuring readers that progress toward better blood sugar control and healthier dessert options, rather than perfection, is the ultimate aim.

SMALL VICTORIES:
Encouraging people to rejoice in each accomplishment, be it learning a new skill or controlling blood sugar while indulging in a sweet treat.

MAINTAINING BALANCE AND MODERATION

MINDFUL INDULGENCE:
Stressing the value of portion management and attentive eating when indulging in desserts to ensure satisfaction without going overboard.

A WELL-BEING LIFESTYLE:
It is urging readers to see dessert as a component of a well-rounded lifestyle that includes regular exercise, stress reduction, and a good diet.

CONTINUED LEARNING AND EXPLORATION

CULINARY CURIOSITY:
Encouraging readers to experiment in the kitchen and satisfy their curiosity by trying out various tastes, ingredients, and preparation methods to increase the variety of desserts they can make that are suitable for people with diabetes.

LIFELONG LEARNING:
Stressing the importance of continuing education and learning about nutrition, cooking, and diabetes control in order to empower people on their path to optimum health.

LOOKING AHEAD WITH OPTIMISM

HOPE FOR THE FUTURE:
As science, technology, and culinary creativity continue to extend possibilities, this article aims to instill optimism and hope for the future of diabetes treatment and dessert enjoyment.

EMPOWERED DECISIONS:
Encouraging people to make knowledgeable decisions regarding their health and well-being while understanding that every choice they make, no matter how minor, has the potential to impact a better future.

Keep Healthier 😊

Thanks. Keep with us.

Printed in Great Britain
by Amazon